Golf: Introduction

IT has been my good fortune and privilege to write on golf for nearly 40 years...from the excitement of reporting on my first Open Championship as a working journalist from Carnoustie in 1975 to the drama of the Ryder Cup at Celtic Manor in 2010.

I have rubbed shoulders with legends, interviewed the leading stars, and witnessed the highs and lows of championship golf. It has been a fascinating journey and one that has given me a rare insight into the world of a sport that captivates millions.

The game of golf is open to everyone – from Tiger Woods to the high handicap hacker. There are no boundaries and age is largely irrelevant.

There are those who describe golf as a waste of a good walk. Clearly, they have not experienced the sense of freedom and enjoyment of a few hours spent trying to put that wee white ball into the hole in as few shots as possible!

Even the most resilient character is driven to the point of distraction at times, but devotees of the Royal & Ancient game invariably keep coming back for more, for golf is highly addictive.

It is also a game littered with great players, great golf courses and great moments, such as Turnberry's Duel in the Sun when Tom Watson and Jack Nicklaus locked horns in arguably the greatest head-to-head ever, which I was fortunate enough to witness.

Hopefully this publication will allow you to enjoy the rich history of golf, from the dawn of the modern game to the present.

Discover the game's origins: why Old Tom Morris was such an influential figure: why St Andrews is the Home of Golf – and also relive the drama of the Duel in the Sun.

This publication has been a labour of love so allow me share with you my great sporting passion.

Put away the clubs, sit back and relax for a few hours and enjoy the experience as you turn the pages to discover all you need to know about golf... **Jim Black**

Publisher **Ken Laird**
Lang Syne Publishers Ltd.
79 Main Street, Newtongrange, Midlothian EH22 4NA
Tel: **0131 344 0414**
E Fax: **0845 075 6085**
E-mail: **info@lang-syne.co.uk**
www.langsyneshop.co.uk
Written by **Jim Black**
Contributer **John Millar**
Design **Dorothy Meikle**
Print **Warners Midlands plc**

FRONT COVER:
Main image:The famous Swilcan Bridge on the Old Course, St Andrews.
© By Graeme Baxter.
Top, left to right: Old Tom Morris.
© Heritage Images/Corbis.
The first golf balls were made of wood.
© Charel Schreuder/Demotix/Corbis
Gleneagles © Graeme Baxter.
Tiger Woods.
© Sam Greenwood/NewSport/Corbis

Golf: An Unsolved Mystery

IT is unclear whether the game of golf originated in China, Rome, Holland or Scotland.

Both the Chinese and the Romans played stick-and-ball games that might be said to have resembled a form of golf, while the Dutch claim that they patented the forerunner to the game we know today.

It is recorded that in February 1297 they played a game with a stick and a leather ball, the object being to hit the ball into a target several hundred yards away in the fewest number of blows.

There are also earlier accounts of a golf-like game being played in continental Europe, which predates the game in Scotland.

A Dutch manuscript from 1261 also refers to a ball game with a colf/kolf club, while in 1360 the council of Brussels banned the game of "colf."

Part of the evidence is that the word "golf" derives from the old Scots terms "golve" or "goff," themselves evolved from the medieval Dutch term "kolf."

The term "kolf" or "kolve" meant club and the Dutch were playing games, mainly on ice, by the 14th Century, where balls were struck by curved sticks. But it might also be argued that such a game is more reminiscent of ice hockey than golf.

Interestingly, the Dutch and the Scots were trading partners, which adds credence to the claim that the game may have been adapted by the Scots from the earlier Dutch version.

We shall never know for sure. But what is not disputed is that golf roughly as we know it emerged in Scotland in the middle ages.

The earliest known reference to golf in Scotland came from King James II, who, in 1457, issued a proclamation banning the playing of golf, or gowf, and football, as he complained these recreational activities were keeping his archers from their practice.

His successors, James III and James IV each re-issued the edict, but the game continued to be played in defiance of the bans and developed over the centuries until, in 1744, when the first known rules were put down in writing in Edinburgh.

Golf was also described as "an unprofitable sport" and Mary, Queen of Scots was accused by her political enemies of playing the game after her second husband, Lord Darnley, was murdered in 1567.

Although James IV had banned the game by act of parliament, it is said that golf clubs and balls were bought for him in 1502 when he visited Perth and later St Andrews and Edinburgh.

An Edinburgh lawyer also claimed that he played golf on Musselburgh links in March 1672, in which case The Old Links, Musselburgh, is the oldest course in the world.

There is even a story that Mary, Queen of Scots,

Golf was already a well established pastime in Scotland when William Mosman painted this famous oil on canvas around 1749.
It shows the sons of a great Highland chief – James Macdonald, on the right, with his gun and younger brother Alexander, left, with club and ball.

played there in 1567. But the earliest documented evidence of instructions for playing the game were found in the diary of a medical student, Thomas Kincaid, who played at Bruntsfield Links, near Edinburgh University, and at Leith Links.

In his entry for 20 January 1687 he noted that after dinner he went for a game of "golve" and "found the only way of playing at the golve is to stand as you do at fencing with the small sword bending you legs a little and holding the muscles of your legs and back and arms exceeding bent or fixt or stiffe and not at all slacking them in the time you are bringing down the stroak."

The need for a set of universal rules and a code of conduct was recognised by The Company of Gentlemen Golfers – later renamed The Honourable Company of Edinburgh Golfers – which played at Leith Links.

These were written in 1744 and became known as the Leith Rules, now preserved in the National Library of Scotland.

The club's claim to be the oldest was later challenged by The Royal Burgess Golfing Society, stating that it had been formed in 1735.

What is a matter of undisputable record is that The Company of Gentlemen Golfers instigated the first trophy, the Silver Club, in the form of a silver golf club provided as sponsorship by Edinburgh Town Council in what was also the first sponsored event in the history of the game.

The first winner, a surgeon by the name of John Rattray attached a silver ball engraved with his name to the club, beginning a long tradition.

When Rattray joined the Jacobite Rising of 1745 he was imprisoned in Inverness and sentenced to death. But he was saved from the gallows by a fellow golfer, Duncan Forbes of Culloden, Lord President of the Court of Session, who pleaded on Rattray's behalf.

It is claimed that James VI's son, Henry Frederick, Prince of Wales, and his courtiers played golf at Blackheath, London in 1603, from which the Royal Blackheath Golf Club traces its origins.

However, it wasn't until the 18th and early 19th Centuries that golf began to spread outside Scotland, when soldiers, expatriates and immigrants introduced the game to British colonies and elsewhere.

This led to the formation of The Royal Calcutta Golf Club, in 1829, and Pau Golf Club, in south western France, in 1856, the oldest clubs outside Britain.

Around the same time, Allan Robertson, a native of St Andrews, had emerged as a pioneer of the game as golf's first recognised professional.

Robertson, who died at the age of just 43 in 1859, earned a formidable reputation in "money matches" and he and his apprentice Tom Morris were unbeaten at foursomes.

Viewed as "the most famous golfing work of art in the world" this painting by Charles Lees shows the annual Grand Match at St Andrews in Autumn, 1844. The scene is set at the 'Ginger Beer Hole' on the Old Course. Lees began his career as a portrait painter and in this work, which took three years to complete, he painted the true likeness of the actual players and spectators.

Like his father and grandfather before him, Robertson was a caddie of the R&A and a golf ball maker in the town, teaching the younger Morris his trade. He was also the first man to break 80 on the Old Course at a time when most struggled to better 100!

The introduction of the solid "gutty" ball – made from the Malaysian gutta percha tree – to replace the old-style "feathery" – made with feathers in a leather casing – also helped popularise the game.

But it was the coming of the railways, most notably to St Andrews, in 1852, that encouraged the spread of golf.

Clubs also began to spring up in England and by 1880 there were 12, rising to 50 over the next seven years and to over 1000 by 1914. Golf was also widely played in Ireland, Australia, New Zealand, Canada and South Africa by the end of the 19th Century.

The Open Championship was also by then firmly established, having been first staged in 1860, at Prestwick. But it wasn't until 1894 that England hosted an Open, when J.H. Taylor won at St George's, Sandwich.

There is evidence that golf was first played in America in the late 18th Century, but it wasn't until the late 19th Century that the game took a hold in the States.

In 1886, Colonel John Hamilton Gillespie laid out two courses in Sarasota, Florida and eight years later delegates from several clubs met in New York to form what was to become the United States Golf Association.

The rise in the game's popularity was dramatic and by 1932 there were over 1100 clubs affiliated to the USGA. Now that figure stands at close to 11,000.

But rewind to the legendary father and son duo of Old Tom and Young Tom Morris, the dominant figures in the early years of championship golf.

The Morris' won all but four of the first 12 Open Championships between them, each four times. Their closest rival of that early generation of professionals was Willie Park Snr of Musselburgh, also with four victories.

Charles Lees. The Golfers. Scottish National Portrait Gallery.

Park's brother Mungo was champion in 1874, while Willie Jnr went on to win in '87 and '89. In the intervening years Jamie Anderson and Bob Ferguson also entered the record books as three-time winners.

It was not until 1890, when John Ball Jnr, from Hoylake, on Merseyside, became the first amateur to be crowned Open champion that a non-Scot triumphed.

But the home players were never again as dominant following the era of "The Great Triumvirate" of Harry Vardon, a Channel Islander, John Henry Taylor, from Devon, and Earlsferry-born James Braid.

The remarkable trio collected 16 Open Championships and 13 second-place finishes between them and Vardon's six victories – the first in 1896, the last in 1914 – remains a record.

The advent of the US Open in 1895 led to several prominent Scots crossing the Atlantic in pursuit of conquering fresh fields and players from the home of golf won 12 of the first 16 stagings of the world's second oldest major championship.

Willie Anderson, from North Berwick, holds the present day record of three consecutive wins from 1903 to 1905. Others, from Carnoustie, St Andrews and Edinburgh, spread the golfing gospel in the years prior to

and immediately following the First World War.

It was inevitable therefore that America would spawn a new breed of champions and so that was the case in the 1920s and early '30s, when the legendary trio of Walter Hagen, Bobby Jones and Gene Sarazen dominated world golf.

Confirmation that the tide had well and truly turned came in the form of a comprehensive 9½-2½ points defeat for Great Britain by the USA in the inaugural Ryder Cup match in 1927.

It took golf some time to recover from the ravages of the Second World War, when so many courses were decimated by military needs, but when the game did eventually re-assert itself on the international stage, the previous growing American dominance was halted for a time.

Englishmen Henry Cotton and Max Faulkner and Northern Ireland's Fred Daly, along with South African Bobby Locke and Australian Peter Thomson ▶

J.H. Taylor, professional player, course architect – one of "The Great Triumvirate."

Gene Sarazen, the first to win all four majors.

kept the American invaders at bay, with the exception of Sam Snead and Ben Hogan.

Locke's four Open victories between 1949 and '57 were matched by Thomson, in 1954, '55, '56 and '58, but it was in 1961 that golf became truly global when a swashbuckling blond-haired American arrived on the scene to help transform the game and bring it into the TV age.

Already an established star in his own country, the charismatic Arnold Palmer quickly acquired celebrity status with the British crowds, dubbed "Arnie's Army," when they roared him to victory in the 1961 Open at Royal Birkdale and again 12 months later at Troon.

Golf in Britain was entering a lean period and while the top players in the world were full-time on the circuit, the majority of their rivals combined tournament golf with their role as club pros.

Tony Jacklin loosened the American

stranglehold in 1969 by becoming the first Briton for 18 years to be crowned Open champion, also winning the US Open the following year.

But it took the arrival of a young Spaniard in 1979 to kick-start the revolution. His name was Severiano Ballesteros, who quickly became known simply as Seve.

Seve's success in the Open at Royal Lytham preceded him becoming the then youngest Masters champion the following year at the age of just 23.

The likes of Jack Nicklaus and Tom Watson were still prominent, but Seve was the catalyst that led to a remarkable upsurge in the fortunes of European golf.

Sandy Lyle, Nick Faldo, Bernhard Langer and Ian Woosnam followed by winning majors and collectively, along with Seve, were nicknamed "The Famous Five."

Another Spaniard, Jose Maria Olazabal also became a multiple major winner in the company of Seve, Lyle, Faldo and Langer, while Paul Lawrie was the first native-born Scot for 68 years to raise the Claret Jug aloft, since Tommy Armour, in 1931.

The decision to extend the Ryder Cup beyond British and Irish players to include Europeans in 1979 and Europe's subsequent successes in the

Seve.

Sandy Lyle.

Nick Faldo.

Bernhard Langer.

Ian Woosnam.

Walter Hagen, famed for his colourful outfits and almost arrogant air, was golf's first great showman.

biennial event also did much to enhance the prestige of the game on this side of the pond.

So, too, has the growth of the European Tour, established in 1972, and now responsible for overseeing a multi-million pound international schedule of nearly 50 events in more than 25 different destinations globally.

Golf, like most businesses, has felt the effects of the world-wide recession, but it has weathered the storm relatively unscathed.

The conveyor belt of talent has continued to churn out a raft of outstanding players; Phil Mickelson, Ernie Els, Colin Montgomerie, Padraig Harrington, Adam Scott and Rory McIlroy, to name but a few.

But the name that instantly springs to the mind of any golf fan is that of Tiger Woods, considered by many to be the finest player of all time.

Woods continues to chase Nicklaus' record of 18 majors and history and the record books will be the final arbiter of his greatness.

But what is absolute fact is that Woods has been responsible for propelling the game to new levels of popularity, prestige and riches.

What may have started out as a stick-and-ball game in Roman times is now a worldwide industry worth tens of billions of pounds. ■

F ROM Stromness to Southerness, Dornoch to Dunbar, Scotland is a land rich in golf courses.

The Home of Golf boasts around 500 golf clubs and nearly 600 courses, making it easily the most densely populated golfing real estate on the planet.

Mainland Scotland and the Islands is also recognised as having some of the very finest courses in the world, notably the Old Course, Carnoustie, Muirfield, Royal Troon and Turnberry – the five Open championship venues.

But St Andrews is the jewel in the country's golfing crown with a proliferation of outstanding courses, most notably the world-renowned Old Course, which hosted its first Open Championship in 1873.

The Royal & Ancient Golf club of St Andrews, considered the spiritual home of golf, has administered the game from its imposing clubhouse since 1754.

But do not assume that St Andrews predominates to the exclusion of all else. Fife is rich in alternatives, stretching from Scotscraig in the north to Dunfermline Golf Club in the west of the county.

Venture beyond the Old Course, The New, The Eden, The Jubilee, The Duke's, The Castle and nearby Kingsbarns and explore some of the finest golfing tracks in the world.

In addition to Scotscraig, Ladybank is also a venue for final Open qualifying and has championship status. So, too, does Lundin Links, close to Leven.

The Crail Golfing Society (the seventh oldest golf club in the world) is rightly proud of its dual offering of the venerable Balcomie Links and Craighead Course on a site offering a sweep of coastal views stretching from St Andrews, Dundee and Carnoustie in the north to Muirfield and Edinburgh to the west.

Elie provides another piece of splendid golfing heritage. James Braid, the five-time Open champion, learned to play the game here while growing up in neighbouring Earlsferry, and golf is said to have been played in the East Neuk since the 15th Century.

Head north and cross the River Tay into Dundee and Angus and further gems wait to be unwrapped and savoured.

According to Jack Nicklaus, Carnoustie, which has hosted the Open Championship on seven occasions, the most recent in 2007, is, in his opinion, the most challenging links course in the world.

But while Carnoustie stands alone, there are many other superb venues at Monifieth, Panmure, Arbroath, Dundee's Downfield, Montrose, Forfar, Letham Grange and Edzell, to name but a few.

Visitors to neighbouring Perthshire are equally

Home of The Open – golf's most prestigious competition has been staged here on 28 occasions.

spoiled, not least those who can afford to indulge themselves amid the splendour of the Five Star Gleneagles Hotel, which has attracted the rich and famous for a century and more.

The hotel overlooks the Kings and Queens courses and the Nicklaus-designed PGA Centenary Course.

Auchterarder Golf Club, which adjoins Gleneagles and runs alongside the PGA Centenary Course, is also a popular venue, as is Blairgowrie's Rosemount, Taymouth Castle, Crieff and Pitlochry.

The Central belt boasts several attractive and challenging tracks at Aberfoyle, Callendar, Dunblane, Stirling, Glenbervie, Falkirk, Grangemouth, Linlithgow and Polmont.

Muirfield is the jewel in Edinburgh and the Lothians' crown. "The Honourable Company of Edinburgh Golfers" was founded in Leith in 1744 before moving to Musselburgh and later in 1891 to its present location.

The East Lothian links has since gone on to achieve world status as an Open Championship venue, hosting 11 Amateur Championships and 16 Opens, the most recent in 2013, when American Phil Mickelson was crowned champion.

But while Muirfield is the most instantly recognised of the region's many clubs and outstanding courses, Edinburgh city also has its share of famous clubs at Baberton, Duddingston, Braid Hills, Bruntsfield, Kings Knowe, Liberton, Portobello and Ratho Park, along with Royal Burgess.

There are also testing tracks at Dalmahoy, Gogarburn, Kings Acre and Turnhouse on the outskirts of the city, while residents on the East Lothian coast are spoiled for choice with Archerfield, Craigielaw, Kilspindie, Gullane, Luffness, Longniddry and North Berwick's Glen on offer, in addition to the largely exclusive Renaissance Club.

Dunbar Golf Club is another of East Lothian's championship links and one of the Open qualifying courses when the world's oldest major is played at Muirfield.

The historic town of Musselburgh rivals St Andrews as a golfing Mecca, with Royal Musselburgh Golf Club – founded in 1774 – The Musselburgh Golf Club and Musselburgh Links.

The Open Championship was staged over the Links six times between 1874 and 1889 and visitors can hire a set of hickory clubs and play the course as it was in its heyday.

North Berwick's championship west links located on the Firth of Forth with stunning sea views across to the Bass Rock – a huge volcanic lump – is the 13th oldest club in the world and the third oldest behind St Andrews and Musselburgh still playing over its original fairways.

Another of North Berwick's claims to fame is that former Prime Minister Arthur Balfour is a past captain.

While St Andrews is the beating heart of world golf, Glasgow is the gateway to a rich and varied selection of clubs with the highest concentration of courses in the country.

Playing two rounds a day it would take almost seven weeks to complete the grand tour of greater Glasgow's many and varied courses.

There are an estimated 94, underlining why Glasgow is known as "The dear green place", given the huge swathes of land given over to the Royal & Ancient game.

Few large cities can claim to have a golf course almost bang in its centre, but Haggs Castle is barely a two mile drive from the heart of Scotland's industrial capital, with the M74 motorway bordering the picturesque setting.

A lush parkland course with tree-lined fairways, Haggs has a thriving membership and is of a standard that was considered good enough to host the Glasgow Classic in the early to mid-1980s and the first of the Scottish Opens after an absence of 13 years, in 1986.

The price of a round of golf in Glasgow varies from £12 at one of the council run municipal courses ▶

such as Knightswood – a nine-hole track – to three-figures and the majority of venues have a pay and play facility with visitor packages available at the more upmarket clubs.

Glasgow Golf Club, situated at Killermont, on the north bank of the River Kelvin, and just five miles from the city centre, is the ninth oldest golf club in the world, having been founded in 1787.

Generally referred to as Killermont, the parkland course follows the original line of play to the greensites laid out by Old Tom Morris in 1903 and the venue has hosted many prestigious tournaments.

Interestingly, the Glasgow Golf Club also owns and runs Glasgow Gailes Links which is situated south of Irvine and north of Troon on the Ayrshire coast, approximately a 40 minute drive from the city.

Gailes also offers visitor packages and is the sole Scottish links to be appointed by the R&A to host final Open Championship qualifying for four years from 2014.

Glasgow's golf clubs and courses are many and varied and cover all points of the city, from the quaintly named Rouken Glen to Ruchill, Cathcart Castle to Cowglen and Kings Park to Linn Park.

Listing each would quickly exhaust the confines of space, but it is worth noting at least some of finest real estate to be found at the home of golf.

Cathcart Castle, established in 1895 and where visitors are welcome all year round, is situated in suburban Clarkston and is a James Braid-designed undulating parkland course offering panoramic views of the city and towards the north west and Loch Lomond.

Braid also designed the East Renfrewshire course, a par 70 6,100 yard track a short hop from Cathcart Castle.

A challenging mix of short par-4s and testing par-3s, the setting allows the visitor to peer over the mighty metropolis that is Glasgow to the north, with the southern Highlands providing a scenic backdrop, while to the west the Firth of Clyde reaches out to the open sea.

Cawder Golf Club, located in Bishopbriggs, just 15 minutes from the city centre, has two outstanding Braid-designed courses, namely The Cawder and The Keir, and an A-listed clubhouse.

Both courses are home to a wide variety of wildlife, including deer and buzzards, and the greens are renowned for their speed and true running.

Pollok Golf Club is situated in the spectacular setting of the Pollok Estate which also houses the Burrell Collection and Pollok House, just a short drive from the city.

Laid out by Dr Alister McKenzie, who also designed Augusta National, beware the 70 bunkers!

Crow Wood, formed in 1925, is yet another Braid-

An atmospheric view of Turnhouse, one of the City of Edinburgh's many fine courses.

designed parkland track offering a relatively inexpensive round of golf just 10 minutes from the city centre heading east.

Stretching just a few miles beyond the city boundary sits Mar Hall Golf & Spa resort. Once the home of the Earl of Mar, the scenic course is perhaps the most exclusive in the area.

This attractive stay & play venue, which is also open to visiting green fee players, is located directly along the banks of the River Clyde, with the towering Erskine Bridge at one end of the course.

The course with a scattering of 250 year old chestnut and beech trees has a linksy feel and each of its nine-hole loops has three riverside holes.

For the more adventurous traveller, Glasgow is also the gateway to Ayrshire and its many splendid courses, including world-renowned Turnberry, Royal Troon and Prestwick on Scotland's most picturesque coastline.

While Turnberry is 50 miles from Glasgow, Royal Troon and Prestwick are less than an hour's drive away.

Royal Troon is a private members club with limited access but Turnberry and Prestwick welcome visitors with fat wallets and a respectable handicap.

The three clubs have, between them, hosted the Open Championship nearly 40 times and are a must-visit for the game's historians, given that they form as famous a golfing terrain as any in the world.

It was at Turnberry in 1977 that Tom Watson and Jack Nicklaus fought

out their iconic Duel in the Sun when the breathtakingly beautiful links with stunning views hosted the first of its four Opens.

The views include the rocky outcrop of Ailsa Craig, the imposing 220 acre island that lies 10 miles from the mainland. Colloquially known as "Paddy's Milestone" because of its location between the Firth of Clyde and the Irish Sea, the island was formed from the volcanic plug of an extinct volcano.

Prestwick, one of the most natural links courses, was the birthplace of the world's oldest major championship, hosting the first 12 Open Championships from 1860.

Other Ayrshire gems include Largs, Bellisle at Ayr, Irvine and West Kilbride, while Renfrewshire and Lanarkshire are rightly proud of Kilmacolm, Ranfurly Castle and Lanark Golf Clubs.

Regrettably, Loch Lomond Golf Club, approximately 35 miles from Glasgow, is exclusively a members club and just about the only way to sample the delights of one of the west of Scotland's most stunning courses is to know one of its well-healed patrons.

The venue for the Scottish Open for 15 years from 1996, Loch Lomond undoubtedly figures on the wish-list of those who "collect" famous golf clubs.

But while Loch Lomond is a "closed shop" to all but the rich and famous, there is a worthwhile alternative to viewing the delights of one

of the world's best known stretches of water a 30 minute drive from Glasgow.

The Carrick on Loch Lomond is a heathland course that weaves through an area of outstanding natural beauty, straddling the imposing Scottish Lowlands and the majestic Highlands.

And if you are planning to sample all 94 of Greater Glasgow's courses before venturing further afield into Ayrshire, allow yourself a couple of months to enjoy the golfing experience of a lifetime.

Island hoppers are spoiled for choice when they visit Arran, described as Scotland in miniature, with no fewer than seven courses, including Shiskine's delightful and unusual 12-hole links.

Machrihanish's championship links is a three-hour drive from Glasgow, but Argyll and Bute's most famous course is worth the effort.

Situated on the western side of the remote Kintyre peninsula and offering views of stunning sunsets, Machrihanish came into being in 1876 and is considered to be one of the most natural and romantic places in the whole of Britain to play golf. ▶

It also has one of the most daunting opening tee shots in golf, a nerve-jangling par 4 with an elevated tee on the edge of the shore. The fairway hugs the beach and you must drive across it with the beach in play.

There are also blind tee shots, fabulous sea views and undulating rippling fairway and exciting rugged dunes. Is it any wonder that the Australian Greg Norman, winner of two Open Championships, made a pilgrimage by helicopter to play there?

The opening of Machrihanish Dunes added to the region's appeal, while nearby Southend, Helensburgh and Dunoon have long established clubs, as do the Islands of Bute, Colonsay, Gigha, Islay, Mull and Tiree.

The Western Isles and Skye also have their share of golfing real estate on Barra, Harris, Lewis and South Uist, with the latter's Askernish perhaps the pick of the bunch.

First laid out by Old Tom Morris in 1891, Askernish has recently been restored using traditional design principle, leading environmental experts to hail it as "the most natural links course in the world."

A two hour sail north of John O Groats, Orkney has a choice of three golf clubs while even further afield, the Shetland Islanders can play on four courses.

Arrive back in Aberdeen on the Shetland Ferry and disembark to a host of golfing riches, starting with Royal Aberdeen, just a few miles from the commercial hub of the Granite City.

The Braid-designed links running along the North Sea shoreline has staged several leading tournaments, including the Senior British Open.

Aberdeen and Aberdeenshire has a proud tradition of golf and the recently opened Trump International Links is already regarded as one of the finest in the world.

Financed by the American business tycoon Donald Trump, the course occupies a three-mile stretch of the North Sea coastline between Murcar Links and Cruden Bay.

Among the very many fine courses are ones at Aboyne, Alford, Banchory, Ballater, Braemar, Cruden Bay, Fraserburgh, Inverurie, Kintore, Meldrum House, Murcar, Portlethen and Peterhead, with Royal Deeside and Balmoral Castle also offering some of the most stunning scenery in the country.

A drive through the spectacular Cairngorm Mountains leads to a proliferation of Highland delights ranging from links to parkland, many of championship standard.

Aviemore, Scotland's ski centre, has the Macdonald Spey Valley Golf Club, home of the European Challenge Tour's Scottish Hydro Challenge for the past several years, while nearby challenging Boat of Garten in the heart of the Cairngorm National Park offers visitors the chance to escape to

With Pollok House and Estate as backdrop Pollok Golf Club is a Glasgow favourite.

the country and savour a true gem surrounded by birch trees, heather and broom.

Every golfing taste is catered for on a Highland tour stretching from the Cairngorms to the Moray Firth, west to Ullapool and Fort William, and far beyond into the furthermost northern region of the country.

It is impossible to travel more than a few miles without having the chance to sample one of the dozens of courses spread across the Highlands, Morayshire, Sutherland, Caithness and all points north, whether it be Brora, Cawdor Castle, Carrbridge, Elgin, Forres, Golspie, Grantown on Spey, Lossiemouth, Newtonmore, Tain, Thurso or Wick.

One of the most picturesque tracks is the one at Fortrose & Rosemarkie, another of the many courses re-designed by Braid and which celebrated its 125th anniversary in 2013.

Situated in the Black Isle, Fortrose offers stunning views over the Moray Firth, close to the Highland capital of Inverness, home of the Scottish Open from 2011 to 2013 at Castle Stuart.

Nairn Golf Club, a half-hour drive from Inverness, was created from a Highland wilderness of gorse and heather and was founded in 1887. It has been as high as number nine in the definitive list of Scotland's top 100 courses and has hosted many tournaments, including the Walker Cup in 1999 and the 2012 Curtis Cup, while silent movie legend Charlie Chaplin extended the town's fame by holidaying there for many years.

© Dennis Hardley Photography

No golfing excursion to the Highlands is complete without a visit to Royal Dornoch, a timeless setting, wild, isolated and, at the same time, stunningly beautiful. The pure white sands divide the links from the Dornoch Firth.

A spellbinding course, which has hosted numerous championships, it has attracted amateurs and professionals alike over the years, including five-time Open champion Tom Watson.

Nearby Skibo Castle, once the home of the billionaire Andrew Carnegie, may be out of the financial reach of the average golfer, but a trip there to sample the delights of the fairytale setting will make you feel temporarily like a millionaire!

Dumfries, Galloway and the Borders is a six hour drive south but it's worth the effort to experience a variety of challenging courses across the region.

Southerness Golf Club on the Solway coast has hosted a variety of championships, from the Scottish Amateur Championship to the Scottish Ladies Championship and is regarded as one of the most testing and attractive of the more modern courses, having been established as recently as 1947.

Visit the peaceful settings of the ruins of Melrose, Kelso, Dryburgh and Jedburgh Abbeys and you'll also chance on a golf course.

One of the best known in the area is the Roxburghe, a parkland course set in a 200 acre estate. A long championship stretch filled with bunkers and lakes, Colin Montgomerie described it as "perfect for professionals and amateurs."

Visitors to the region are again spoiled for choice. In addition to the Dumfries & Galloway, the Dumfries & County and Crichton Golf Club in the county town, there are fine courses at Castle Douglas, Dalbeattie, Galashiels, Gatehouse of Fleet, Kelso, Langholm, Lauder, Lochmaben, Lockerbie, Newton Stewart, Peebles and Portpatrick.

Coldstream, Eyemouth, Sanquhar, Selkirk, Stranraer, St Boswells and Wigtown are among many other towns offering first class facilities.

Those wishing to wine and dine after a demanding 18 holes can also enjoy the luxury of the Macdonald Cardrona at Peebles and the Cally Palace at Gatehouse of Fleet.

It is impossible to give every golf club in Scotland a name check due to the constraints of space, but hopefully readers have enjoyed a flavour of exactly why Scotland is indeed the Home of Golf. ■

In a survey 80 per cent
of golfers admitted cheating.
The other 20 per cent lied. – *Bruce Lansky*

We were all born with webbed
feet and a golf club in our hand.
*– Old Tom Morris referring to people
born on the east coast of Scotland*

They call it golf because all the other
four letter words were taken.
– Ray Floyd

If you are caught on a golf course
during a storm and are afraid
of lightning, hōld up a 1-iron.
Not even God can hit a 1-iron.
– Lee Trevino

The only time my prayers are never
answered is on the golf course.
– Billy Graham

A Slice of Heaven

I T is impossible to define just a select few of the world's tens of thousands of golf courses as the finest on the planet.

But it seems reasonable to assume that few would decline the chance to begin a tour of some of Britain and Ireland's most famous links at the "Home of Golf" before venturing across the Atlantic to complete the journey at Augusta and Pebble Beach. ▶

Augusta

Turnberry

Waterville

Carnoustie

Royal Troon

Pebble Beach

Images © Graeme Baxter

Graeme Baxter is the official artist to some of the world's most important golf tournaments, such as The Ryder Cup, The Open Championship, The Presidents Cup and The Kraft Nabisco Championship, as well as artist to the PGA Tour and European Tour. With his work displayed in clubhouses at St Andrews, Augusta, Pebble Beach, Dubai, Mission Hills and Pine Valley in China, Graeme possesses a unique ability to historically record golf landscapes and portraits that capture his passion for the game. For information on buying prints please go to the website **www.GraemeBaxter.com** and for more information email **Sales@GraemeBaxter.com** or the UK Distributer **BaxterGolfArt@CachetUK.com**

15

The Old Course St Andrews

RECOGNISED universally as "The Home of Golf", there is no definitive record of who created the original Old Course, but Mother Nature undoubtedly had a large say in laying out the most iconic links in world golf.

The Jewel in Scotland's golfing crown was founded in 1764 when the original design of 22 holes – 11 out and 11 back – was reduced to 18, the standard number we have today.

Old Tom Morris and Alister Mackenzie subsequently redesigned the Old Course in turn, but both remained true to its natural lay-out that has bewitched generations of amateurs and professionals alike.

The venue is also home to the Royal & Ancient Golf Club of St Andrews, referred to generally as the R & A, golf's governing body responsible for the Rules of Golf, and the world-famous clubhouse headquarters overlooks the 1st tee and the 18th green.

Recognised as the most demanding test of golf of any of the established championship courses, the Old Course hosted its first Open in 1873 and has staged a further 27 since, the most recent in 2010, when the South African, Louis Oosthuizen was crowned champion.

A Mecca for all golfers regardless of ability, the links are public and run by a trust. Moreover, no play is allowed on Sundays with the exception of major tournaments.

Until the late 1890s, when Old Tom Morris widened the fairways and created larger greens so they could hold two flags, golfers played out and back to the same holes. Even now, only a handful of holes have their own greens – most notably the 1st, 9th, 17th and 18th – with the rest sharing huge double greens.

A formidable test for even the most accomplished player, the Old Course is peppered with intimidating bunkers, perhaps the most notorious being "Hell" bunker, the largest, on the par-5 14th hole.

Not to everyone's liking because it is so hard to read, the Old Course's closing stretch features some of the most instantly recognisable landmarks in world golf, including the renowned "Swilcan Bridge," the ancient stone bridge over the burn that runs in front of the first green.

The hopes of many of the game's greatest players have floundered at the penultimate "Road Hole" which immediately precedes the most photographed 18th green on the planet, protected by the "Valley of Sin," a deep swale that draws the ball like a magnet.

To sum up, the Old Course is quirky, demanding and at times infuriating, but, with the constantly changing conditions, it is most certainly never predictable or boring!

Graeme W Baxter 05.

Turnberry Ayrshire, Scotland

THE south Ayrshire links is most famous for golf's Duel in the Sun, the epic final round featuring Tom Watson and Jack Nicklaus at the first of Turnberry's four Opens in 1977.

The pair went head-to-head in glorious July sunshine in one of the most absorbing duels in the game's history between the two greatest players of their generation.

Needing to match Nicklaus' birdie on the 18th to claim the Claret Jug for a second time, Watson duly did so to clinch victory.

Fast forward 32 years and by a quite remarkable quirk of fate Watson was on the cusp of a sixth Open triumph at the age of 59 when he missed an eight foot putt for bogey at the last, resulting in a play-off, which he lost to fellow American Stewart Cink, at the same time adding to Turnberry's mystique.

Opened for play in 1901, Turnberry's original design was by Willie Fernie. Changes were made to the lay-out by Major C.K. Hutchinson 37 years later and but for the advent of the Second World War, Turnberry would very probably have remained as the latter envisaged it in 1938.

The peace and tranquillity of the picturesque Ayrshire coast was initially shattered by the First World War, when the hotel and golf courses were taken over for military training.

But the outbreak of hostilities in 1939 had a much more devastating effect on Turnberry. The Royal Air Force built an airfield mostly on the old Arran Course, but also affecting what became the Ailsa championship course.

In an effort to restore the links to its former glory, course architect Philip Mackenzie Ross was employed to redesign the lay-out, creating what is today regarded as one of the finest pieces of golf real estate in the world.

Although criticised by some as lacking the challenge and grandeur of the Old Course or Carnoustie, Turnberry is nonetheless regarded as demanding track and a prime location with magnificent sea views, notably the extinct volcanic rock known as Ailsa Craig that rises majestically from the Firth of Clyde.

There is also the ruin of Bruce's Castle, home of Robert 1 of Scotland in his formative years, and the world-famous Lighthouse adjacent to the ninth tee.

Turnberry's tough four-five-four finish sets it apart from many of its rivals and the closing three holes have been the downfall of many of the world's finest players.

American property tycoon Donald Trump acquired ownership of Turnberry in April, 2014, and announced plans to make several changes to the Ailsa course.

Carnoustie Angus, Scotland

JACK NICKLAUS believes Carnoustie to be one of the greatest tests of links golf anywhere in the world and he is not alone among the legends of the game in lauding the course where they have played golf for more than 170 years.

The advent of a rail link as far back as 1838 added to the town's popularity as a visitor centre and a local, Robert Chambers had the foresight to create a golf course.

But it was under Allan Robertson's eye for design that Carnoustie evolved. One of the early pioneers of professionalism, Robertson revised his initial 10-hole lay-out over a period of years before others made further changes.

Old Tom Morris, Bob Simpson, James Braid and James Wright all had a hand in creating the course we know today, the latter having been responsible for the three-hole closing stretch that can strike terror in the hearts of the unwary and inattentive.

The club was successful in persuading the R&A to stage the 1931 Open on its links. Carnoustie has subsequently hosted six more championships, most recently in 2007, when Padraig Harrington was crowned champion.

Tommy Armour, Henry Cotton, Ben Hogan, Gary Player, Tom Watson and Paul Lawrie preceded Harrington as champions, but only Hogan can be said to have come close to taming the monster that has been nicknamed "Carnastie" with a near flawless final round in 1953 and a four-shot victory.

In 1999 the Frenchman Jean van de Velde contrived to throw away the title when he chose to try to play out of the infamous Barry Burn at the last instead of electing to play safe and lost in a play-off to Lawrie, who had made up a ten shot deficit in the final round.

The burn guarding the final green has been the source of much drama over the years and it makes Carnoustie's 18th a true test of nerve and one of the most intimidating finishes in world golf.

Carnoustie's many hazards, including the Spectacles double bunkers carved into a hillside on the 14th, and "blind" shots are a test for the most accomplished player, given that even the smallest of errors is invariably punished.

But the aforementioned Hogan refused to be intimidated by the challenge. The American legend played the 578-yard par-5 sixth to such perfection four times in a row, flirting with the out-of-bounds on each occasion, that they named it Hogan's Alley.

Put simply, Carnoustie is an exacting challenge and an exciting examination calling for mental strength and unwavering attention.

Graeme W Baxter 07

21

Royal Troon Ayrshire, Scotland

R OYAL TROON was a work in progress for 10 years from 1878 before it became a proper 18 hole golf course and it took a further 35 years to improve the lay-out sufficiently to create the basis of the great championship links we know today.

George Strath and Willie Fernie were responsible for the original draft, but it was five-time Open champion James Braid who supplied the final touches in terms of lengthening the course and improving the greens in preparation for the first major championship to be staged there in 1923.

Since that momentous occasion, Royal Troon has hosted seven more Opens, most recently in 2004, when the unsung American Todd Hamilton was the unlikely champion, defeating the much more vaunted Ernie Els in a play-off.

In some senses, at first glance Royal Troon is the least appealing of the Open venues, lacking neighbouring Turnberry's panoramic splendour and Muirfield's need for exact precision. But a closer examination reveals that it possesses some great holes.

There is also an element of quirkiness about Royal Troon, in particular the world-famous "Postage Stamp", the par-3, 123 yard eighth hole, where the American Gene Sarazen, known as "The Squire", had a hole-in-one during the 1973 Open at the age of 71.

He was the oldest person ever to score one in a major. Incredibly, Scot David Russell became the youngest 45 minutes earlier, when he also claimed an ace.

Willie Park Jnr is credited with giving the hole its name after describing it as "a pitching surface skimmed down to the size of a postage stamp."

But allow your ball to slip off the surface and it will leave you in either some of Britain's deepest bunkers, with near vertical faces, or one of the many hollows for which Royal Troon is famous.

In 1997, Tiger Woods' hopes of a first Open victory floundered at the "Postage Stamp", where he ran up a triple-bogey six to drop out of contention.

It's rumoured that at least some of Royal Troon's hazards were created by soldiers who used the area for hand-grenade practice during the Second World War and they are to blame for the seemingly bottomless pits.

South African Bobby Locke and Americans Arnold Palmer, Tom Weiskopf, Tom Watson and Justin Leonard are among Royal Troon's Open champions.

A private member's club, Royal Troon is also where eight-time European number one Colin Montgomerie, a resident in the town, perfected his game.

Graeme W Baxter 04

Gleneagles Perthshire, Scotland

THE world-famous Gleneagles Hotel boasts three championship courses, The King's, The Queen's and the PGA Centenary.

While the King's and Queen's have been in existence for almost 100 years and have attracted a host of international stars, including Hollywood legends Bing Crosby, Burt Lancaster and Sean Connery, as well as astronaut Alan Shepard – the only man to hit a golf shot on the moon – they have been upstaged by the youngest of the trio.

Designed by Jack Nicklaus, the PGA Centenary Course was chosen to host the 2014 Ryder Cup on its return to Scotland for the first time for 41 years.

Opened for play in 1993, even a champion and course architect of Nicklaus' standing found the design extremely challenging.

Describing it as "the finest parcel of land in the world I have ever been given to work with", Nicklaus eventually created a masterpiece.

The tees are graded at each hole in five stages and the course begins by playing southwest towards the glen, sweeping up to the Ochil Hills to the summit of the pass below Ben Shee.

The feature of the PGA Centenary Course is the feast of views of the spectacular countryside in which Gleneagles is set.

Putting on the two-tier second green, you are distracted by the lush panorama. As you move westward over the next few holes, the rugged Grampian Mountains come into view on the right, then distantly, Ben Vorlich and the mountains above the Trossachs.

The course, which hosts the Johnnie Walker Championship annually on the European Tour, underwent extensive renovations, in particular installing new drainage, including SubAir systems on all the greens, and rebuilt bunkers using cutting edge technology ahead of the Ryder Cup.

But the most noticeable changes involved a major revamp of the 18th in an effort to produce a more spectacular finish to the previously much-maligned closing hole. The tee box was raised to provide better visibility off the fairway and the final 250 yards were entirely redone involving the lowering of the fairway by five metres and the green rebuilt as well as several surrounding bunkers.

While the first official Ryder Cup match was staged in 1927, golf historians point out that a match was played in 1921 at Gleneagles (on the King's Course) which featured the best American players to compete in an international match against a British team.

The match was the brainchild of the *Glasgow Herald* newspaper and the British team featuring such greats as Harry Vardon and J.H. Taylor triumphed 9-3 in front of a large and enthusiastic crowd.

Graeme W Baxter 196

THE stunning beauty of the course's surroundings, with Loch Lomond and the Bonnie Banks on one side and Ben Lomond on the other make this one of the most spectacular tracks in world golf.

Opened in 1993, Loch Lomond hosted the Scottish Open in various guises from 1996 to 2010 prior to the event being switched to Castle Stuart Golf Club, Inverness and was regularly featured worldwide on television.

Loch Lomond's status on the international stage was further enhanced when it also hosted the biennial Solheim Cup match between Europe and the United States in 2000.

There has also been repeated talk of the venue staging a World Golf Championship event at a future date.

The initial project to create a world class parkland course ran into financial difficulties and was rescued from bankruptcy by American businessman Lyle Anderson in 1994, five years after former Open champion Tom Weiskopf and Jay Morrish had laid out their design.

While work is continually ongoing to improve the experience of a truly great course, Loch Lomond in its present form is guaranteed to take the breath away and the dramatic backdrop is also likely to prove a huge distraction to even the most focussed player.

But there is a need for clear thinking on a course that calls for careful thought and strategic planning, starting at the first where an ancient oak tree on the right-hand side can prove off-putting although it is less troublesome than it appears at first sight.

After the first five holes, the Loch on the right-hand side opens up at the sixth known as Long Loch Lomond, a 625-yard challenge for even the most accomplished players, followed by Yon Bonnie Banks, Inchmoan and Shi G'Arten before turning back inland for the back nine on the western half of the course, where the distractions are the wildlife, the bogs and abandoned buildings.

The challenge also changes with a mixture of uphill and downhill drives, notably the 11th which is a long uphill short hole requiring sound judgement as well as brute strength and the 14th – the Weiskopf-Morrish signature hole – short par-4, where Weiskopf became trapped in a peat bog for several hours during construction.

The 205-yard 17th brings the player back to water in peaceful Rossdhu Bay with its lochside green before the closing challenge of bunkers on the right and water down the left at the closing hole with its green in the shadow of the ruin that is Rossdhu Castle.

THE Southport links has undergone constant changes since its inception in 1889 but it has retained its dunescape look created by a sea of sand sweeping in from the Lancashire coast.

Seven years after the creation of the golf club, the members sought out a new and larger site to the south of the original nine-hole course, but it wasn't until 1909 that the Birkdale we know today came into being when George Lowe designed an 18-hole track.

Frederick Hawtree and J.H. Taylor then put their minds to upgrading the venue as a championship course in the 1930s before further alterations were made by the former's son, Fred 30 years later.

A third generation of the famous Hawtree family of course architects, Martin supervised the reconstruction of the greens in 1990 and repositioned five of the championship tees to improve their line.

He carried out additional improvements between 2004 and 2007, removing 12 fairway bunkers and adding 16 new ones, by which time Royal Birkdale had become an established Open Championship venue.

The first of these was held in 1954, when the Australian, Peter Thomson won the first of three successive titles.

The Open has returned on a further eight occasions, most recently in 2008, when Irishman Padraig Harrington completed a back-to-back "double."

When Arnold Palmer won in 1961 they erected a plaque on the course on the spot on the 16th fairway, where he smashed a remarkable 6-iron shot onto the green in the second round, to the astonishment of onlookers.

Described as a "stadium-style" links and noted as a fair but demanding test of golf, Royal Birkdale is swathed in huge piles of sand and wild grasses and is regarded as one of the most spectacular courses in the world.

The greens have undulating surfaces rather than severe slopes and the art of green-reading is an important factor in determining success or failure.

The landmark brilliant white Art Deco clubhouse stands out like a beacon, given its unusual design and unique lines.

In addition to the Open, Royal Birkdale has hosted a number of other major champions, including the Amateur Championship, the Walker Cup, the Curtis Cup, the Women's British Open, the Senior British Open and the Ryder Cup, twice, in 1965 and 1969.

Royal Birkdale also lies within a Site of Special Scientific Interest and the open, rolling landscape is a haven for birds and other wildlife.

Graeme W Baxter 08

MORE commonly referred to as Hoylake, Royal Liverpool Golf Club is England's second oldest course and is steeped in history.

Built in 1869 on the racecourse of the Liverpool Hunt Club, Hoylake was designed by Robert Chambers and George Morris and extended to 18 holes two years later, when the club was accorded "Royal" status through the patronage of Queen Victoria's younger son, the Duke of Connaught.

Hoylake staged the first international match between England and Scotland in 1892 and also hosted the inaugural showdown between Great Britain and the United States in 1921, in what was the forerunner to the Walker Cup.

The rules of the amateur game were also laid down at Hoylake and its most famous member, John Ball – one of only three amateurs to win the Open – went on to be the Amateur Champion eight times.

Another Hoylake player, Harold Hilton was crowned Open champion on his home course the first time the championship was staged there in 1897, while the legendary Bobby Jones' success in 1930 formed part of his unique grand slam.

In a period of 70 years between 1897 and 1967, Hoylake was the venue for a total of nine Opens won by Hilton, Sandy Herd, Arnaud Massy, J.H. Taylor, Walter Hagen, Jones, Fred Daly, Peter Thomson and Roberto de Vicenzo, in turn.

But the growing demands of commercialism outgrew the course and it was another 39 years before the Open returned to the links, which had undergone further changes in its design in the intervening period.

The purchase of an adjacent disused school playing field meant that a site could be found for the necessary infrastructure associated with the championship.

In baking hot temperatures in 2006 Tiger Woods won his third Open title and became the first player since compatriot Tom Watson in 1983 to complete back-to-back victories.

Woods left his driver in the bag and navigated his way round on the baked-hard fairways with his long-irons to clinch an emotional victory just two months after the death of his father, Earl.

Although the course can appear relatively benign and flat, there is an undulating string of holes that run down the side of the shoreline that are a test of skill and patience, most especially when the wind sweeps in off the Irish Sea.

In 2001 three new greens were built and for the 2006 Open major changes were made to the 17th to satisfy the R&A's demands.

Royal St. George's, Sandwich

ARGUABLY the most famous golf course in southern England, Royal St George's – often referred to as simply Sandwich – has hosted a raft of championships during the course of the past 120 years.

In addition to the Amateur Championship, the Walker Cup, the Curtis Cup and the Ladies British Amateur Open, St George's has also staged the Open Championship on no fewer than 12 occasions, the first in 1894 and somewhat more recently in 2011.

Laidlaw Purves and Ramsay Hunter initially laid out the course in 1887 at a cost of £1,000. The links represent seaside golf at its best with the huge sand dunes used to create a natural and spectacular challenge.

J.H. Taylor's winning score of 326 at the first Open testified to the course's level of difficulty and reflected the number of blind shots and Purves' love of cross-hazards. But by the time the Open returned eight years later following the introduction of the rubber-core Haskell ball, the winning ball had been reduced by 30 strokes and changes were required.

The back nine was nearly 600 yards longer than the front nine and significant modifications were carried out to rectify the disparity. These included moving the 10th green atop a dune and the hole later featured in the Ian Fleming James Bond movie *Goldfinger*.

After St George's had hosted its seventh Open in 1949, the R&A decided that the course was no longer of the necessary standard to stage their premier event due to the fact that it was viewed as antiquated.

But in order to attract the return of the Open, course architect Frank Pennick was commissioned to carry out significant changes in 1975. He made major alterations to the third, eight and 11th holes, bringing the two nines to withn 50 yards of each other.

These changes met with the R&A's approval and the 1981 Open was awarded to St George's after an absence of 32 years. It is a measure of the success of Pennick's revamping of the course that the championship also returned four years later and again in 1993.

The sand hills on the front nine are the largest of any Open course and with the exception of the Old Course, the fairways produce the most unpredictable bounces, often to the irritation of the professionals.

It is the perfect combination for championship golf, requiring accurate driving and a precise short game, coupled to a sense of adventure, given the continuing existence of blind shots.

Northern Ireland's Darren Clarke won the most recent Open Championship to be staged at St George's, in 2011, when he prevailed by a margin of three stokes from the American duo of Dustin Johnson and Phil Mickelson to become a major champion for the first time at the age of 42.

Celtic Manor, Newport, Wales

THE 2010 Ryder Cup is the jewel in Celtic Manor's crown, the first to be held in Wales. It was also the realisation of a dream for Sir Terry Matthews, the billionaire local businessman who created the resort.

Having bought the manor house as a £100million redevelopment and refurbishment project in 1980, Matthews opened the Celtic Manor Hotel two years later before turning his attention to building two golf courses.

Robert Trent Jones Sr. was commissioned as designer and work began on the Roman Road Course – named after the main route connecting the Roman fortress of Caerleon with the town of Caerwent which crosses the land – in 1992. A short time later work was started on a £10million clubhouse.

The Coldra Woods course was completed in 1996 and the Wentwood Hills track three years later, but in order to facilitate a bid to stage the Ryder Cup the Twenty Ten Course was built as part of a £16million development, the first course in history to be purpose-built for the event.

Part of the ambitious project involved the building of a 12-metre-long twin-suspension bridge linking the practice ground to the golf course, a new clubhouse and the surrounding infrastructure, as part of the 2001 bid to host the event.

Matthews' Ryder Cup dream was in danger of turning into a nightmare when the course was hit by a deluge, forcing the biennial match into a fourth day for the first time in the history of the Ryder Cup.

But it was a measure of the strength of the Twenty Ten Course that it stood up to the conditions to allow the match to be completed on the Monday, with Europe claiming a 14½-13½ victory after the Americans had staged a dramatic comeback in the singles.

Europe had trailed 6-4 after the opening fourballs and foursomes, but the third session featuring two sets of foursomes and four fourballs resulted in a dramatic American collapse when the visitors won just half a point from a possible six. This meant the hosts led by three overall going into the singles. But the United States clawed their way back and the result hinged on the final match between Graeme McDowell and Hunter Mahan.

The Wentwood Hills course was extensively remodelled to become the Twenty Ten Course opened in 2007, while the Coldra Woods track was replaced by the Montgomerie Course in the same year.

The Twenty Ten Course has a capacity of 50,000 and as well as hosting the Ryder Cup it is also the venue for the Wales Open.

Regarded as the premier resort in Wales, Celtic Manor currently boasts three courses, the Twenty Ten, the Montgomerie and the Roman Road and in 2012 the hotel announced a £160million 10-year plan for developing the complex.

Royal County Down is described as a mix of heaven and hell, beautiful yet at the same time terrifying; a true test of links golf on a course that boasts in excess of 130 bunkers and thick gorse waiting to trap a wayward shot.

Founded in 1900 and designed by Old Tom Morris, little of the original lay-out remains. A member, George Coombe made significant changes and later, in 1926, Harry Colt carried out further alterations to create the course that exists today.

Royal County Down would almost certainly have hosted an Open championship by now but for the political situation in the province, where the security risk was considered too great.

In fact, the Open has been staged only once in Northern Ireland, at Royal Portrush, in 1951, when Englishman Max Faulkner won his only major.

But Royal County Down has hosted numerous other championships, including the Irish Open, the Curtis Cup, the Amateur Championship, the Walker Cup and the senior British Open.

The front nine was described by five-time Open champion Tom Watson "as fine a nine holes as I have ever played" and the home stretch also contains two testing par-3s and a formidable closing hole of 550 yards that features in excess of 20 bunkers.

There is also a proliferation of "blind" holes on a course that is both enthralling and punishing and one that also requires a stroke or two of good fortune.

With the fells of the world-famous Mountains of Mourne as a backdrop and the Irish Sea skirting the links, there is a truly wild beauty about the setting that has attracted the game's top players over the years.

The par-3 fourth hole offers one of the finest views from high among the dunes. It is also one of the trickiest challenges, with 10 bunkers in play calling for a well directed shot to hold the putting surface.

With its deep hollows, intimidating array of bunkers, spectacular scenery and downhill lies calling for patience, a steady nerve and precision, Royal County Down fits the identikit of a truly great course, as was demonstrated at the 2007 Walker Cup, when the competition went down to the very last match before the Americans clinched victory.

That Royal County Down would be capable of hosting an Open Championship is without doubt and the fact that the R&A has taken the Senior British Open there several times suggests the venue is at least in their thoughts.

B UT for an Irish-American philanthropist, Waterville would almost certainly have remained a largely forgotten former company town tucked away on the stunningly beautiful Ring of Kerry.

Back in the late 1880s, Waterville became a thriving community after being chosen as the eastern landfall for a transatlantic telephone cable.

With the sudden influx of workers came the demand for recreational facilities and a basic nine-hole golf course was constructed to partially meet their needs.

But the company and the course had long since closed down when exceedingly rich expatriate John Mulcahy visited the area in the 1970s with a vision to create a prime slice of golfing real estate on the original site.

Forty years on, Mulcahy's creation is recognised as one of the finest examples of a modern golf course constructed with the use of spectacular dunes, bunkers, sand hills, a river and low hillocks in the shadow of the famed Macgillicuddy's Reeks, with the Atlantic waters on one side.

Mulcahy worked with course designer Eddie Hackett to turn his dream into reality and, in 2003, Tom Fazio, recognised as an outstanding architect of new courses and a renovator of existing great ones, contributed to Waterville's appeal by adding further drama to the holes.

Waterville has yet to attract a world-class tournament, due largely to its remoteness, but that has not stopped a clutch of top players from visiting the links and admiring the magnificent test of golf, particularly before the Open, among them Tiger Woods, Jim Furyk and the late Payne Stewart.

Indeed, Stewart fell in love with the links and the local surroundings and had just agreed to become the honorary captain for the year 2000 when he tragically died in a plane crash only months after winning his second US Open.

But such was the affection of the locals for the American Ryder Cup star that a bronze statue of him leaning on his putter was erected behind the ninth green.

Another of the game's legends, Sir Henry Cotton described Waterville as one of the greatest courses ever built, adding: "If it were located in Britain it would undoubtedly be a venue for the British Open."

A combination of terrifying par fours and fives and challenging par-3s, Waterville's closing hole is close to 600 yards long and is regarded as one of the great finishing holes of golf, with the beach on one side and a series of daunting bunkers on the left completed by a tricky green.

Kerry, Republic of Ireland

Old Head Golf Links   County

OLD HEAD is situated on a 220 acre diamond-shaped area that extends two miles out into the Atlantic Ocean and is over 7,200 yards long. Located on the southern tip of Ireland it is both remote and still accessible. Some have described it as "the edge of the world".

The green complexes for each hole have been designed to be as open as possible, thus offering the player a view of the ocean from every hole. The lay-out effectively creates a 360 degree panoramic view from this stunning perch high above the water.

Located in County Cork on the southwest coast, Old Head was the brainchild of brothers John and Patrick O'Connor and was opened for play in 1997. But despite having been in existence for only a short time, the course seems to fit the land so naturally that it appears to have been there forever.

The owners wanted very much to have a walking course and the walkways utilise the natural surroundings to offer the most powerful views. The second hole is where the seaside walk starts and you are often walking right beside the incredible cliffs before being directed back to the fairway.

Those who suffer from vertigo might find some of the tees present a problem, given they are 300 feet up. It is also advisable to take a plentiful supply of balls as there is little margin for error on the holes bordering the cliff tops.

It would be difficult to replicate this track anywhere else and the area also offers diverse ecology and wildlife as well.

The sense of history at Old Head is also overwhelming. There are many man-made structures including the remains of a lighthouse built in 1667. The current lighthouse was built in 1853 and just off shore are the sites of many famous shipwrecks including the sinking in 1915 of the *Lusitania* by a German torpedo, one of the most pivotal moments in 20th Century history.

A number of people were involved in the creation of Old Head including Dr Joe Carr, Ireland's most famous amateur player.

There is an ancient burial ground at the approach to the 10th but there are many memorable holes, none more so than the 17th called the Lighthouse. It's a long par-5 requiring a bold second shot to the right side of the fairway. Anything left will leave a blind shot to the green which is nestled in a punchbowl on the edge of the cliffs.

The 18th is a dramatic closing hole that should be played from the high back tees for maximum drama. The fourth, hewn out of natural rock and overlooked by the lighthouse, was described by Joe Carr as the razor's edge and sweeps for 430 yards along the Old Head. It has a generous fairway but the second shot needs to be accurate to find the green.

Cork, Republic of Ireland

Augusta National   Augusta,

Purely man-made, Augusta National is perhaps second only to the Old Course in terms of its status as the home of the The Masters.

Generally regarded as the second most prestigious major after the Open, the Masters is the only one of golf's big four to have a permanent home.

The brainchild of arguably the greatest amateur to play the game, Augusta is Bobby Jones' lasting legacy to the game he graced with such distinction, winning 13 majors before retiring from competitive play at the at the age of just 28.

A native of Atlanta, Jones somewhat surprisingly chose to locate his world-class course in Augusta on a site that had previously housed a nursery known as Fruitlands.

He employed the renowned course architect Dr Alister MacKenzie to design his dream track but it is generally held that Jones had a significant input and emphasised the importance of strategy over power.

The wider fairways, the absence of rough and a minimal number of bunkers highlighted Jones' desire to make Augusta a more attractive proposition for the less skilled player by creating room to hit the ball offline.

At the same time Augusta is a challenging proposition for the professionals to plot their way strategically round finding the right locations to aggressively attack the pins.

By 1934, Jones had inaugurated the Augusta National Invitational Tournament, which quickly grew into The Masters.

Over the years Augusta has evolved and is very different from the course Jones envisaged, both in length and degree of difficulty.

The most famous stretch is Amen Corner, the 11th, 12th and 13th holes, which have somewhat changed from their original design.

Amen Corner can end in water torture for some with a small pond a feature of the 11th while the 12th green – a treacherous short par-3 – is angled behind Rae's Creek, a tributary of which also flanks the 13th.

The famed Eisenhower tree on the 17th, so named for President Dwight Eisenhower, whose tee shots had a habit of knocking on wood, is now gone, the victim of ice damage caused by extreme weather conditions, but the sloping greens and the various hazards make Augusta the ultimate test of nerve and skill.

The exclusive property of home players for the first 24 stagings of the The Masters, South African Gary Player eventually ended the American stranglehold in 1961.

But only 13 non-Americans have earned the right to wear the Green Jacket. They include Scotland's Sandy Lyle, Englishman Nick Faldo and Welshman Ian Woosnam.

42

Georgia, USA

Pebble Beach California, USA

DESCRIBED by some as the greatest public course in the world, Pebble Beach has hosted the US Open on five occasions, the last time as recently as 2010, when Northern Ireland's Graeme McDowell was crowned champion.

Situated less than a mile from Cypress Point on the Monterey Peninsula, Pebble, as it is affectionately referred to, features a sequence of seven holes from the fourth to the tenth that have the Pacific Ocean as their backdrop.

The course was laid out in 1919, as part of the resort complex owned by the Del Monte fruit company and owes its design to the duo of Jack Neville and Douglas Grant.

Given its setting, Pebble is as nature intended and little has changed over the years although Jack Nicklaus was commissioned to create a new fifth hole in 1998.

Previously the hole had always played inland as the owners of a beachfront property had refused to sell. But, finally, in 1995, the company managed to acquire the land and now the seaside sequence is unbroken.

The sixth to the 10th is widely regarded as the toughest five-hole run in golf and when the wind blows even the top players are in the laps of the gods.

Any shot veering right at the sixth invariably ends up in the Pacific and big numbers are commonplace, while, the seventh, a short par-3, is optically deceptive as the shortest hole in major championship golf and easy to misjudge distance-wise, with the obvious risk of playing too long through the green or being a club short.

The eighth is a dramatic tee shot high over an ocean inlet and the ninth has a deep cliff down the right hand side, where anything short or left will probably find the deep gully.

The 10th also has cliffs on the right and the presence of a large bunker complex on the sloping fairway is an added challenge further complicated by a deep ravine front right of the green.

Away from the ocean, the fairways sweep through pines and cypress trees and are a little easier by comparison. But even in perfect weather conditions, Pebble is a challenging track.

But for all its intimidating properties, Pebble is regarded as one of the truly great courses in world golf, with Nicklaus once claiming: "If I had one last round to play, I would likely choose Pebble Beach. It's possibly the best in the world."

And 2-time Major champ Johnny Miller added: "Pebble is a piece of sacred ground. They say its the greatest meeting of land and water in the world."

OPENED in 1928, Cypress Point is a delightful mix of rocky coastline, massive sand dunes and lush forests, everything you could want in a golf course.

The brainchild of a woman, Marion Hollis, the 1921 US Women's Amateur champion, Cypress Point was bankrolled by a syndicate of financiers. Hollis had moved west from New York to work in real estate when she spotted the potential to create an outstanding golf course on the parcel of land on the Monterey coastline.

It was Hollis who appointed renowned course architect Mr Alister MacKenzie and Robert Hunter to turn her vision into reality.

But Mackenzie was not her first choice. That honour went to Seth Raynor, who died before the project had begun taking shape. So Hollis turned to MacKenzie.

On taking over the project, Mackenzie decided to discard all previous plans and instead devised his own routing based on three key objectives.

These were to create the finishing stretch of holes near to, or directly alongside, the ocean for dramatic effect, feature holes woven in and out of the dunes and forest throughout the round, giving the lay-out an adventurous, ever-changing feel, and, finally, utilising a single sand dune as an attractive backdrop for no fewer than four holes, the third, sixth, ninth and 11th.

Mackenzie, ably assisted by his partner, Hunter, said of the finished article which included 125 bunkers: "For years I have been contending that in our generation no other golf course could possibly compete with the strategic problems, the thrills, excitement, variety and lasting and increasing interest of the Old Course, but the completion of Cypress Point has made me change my mind."

Regarded as unorthodox, Cypress Point features back-to-back par-5s at the fifth and sixth and par-3s at the 15th and 16th.

The closing stretch of 15, 16 and 17 also hang above the Pacific in what is regarded as one of the most aesthetically pleasing experiences in world golf.

The 16th with its bunker-ringed green at the beginning of a rocky headland represents a blend of beauty, challenge and strategy.

But, regrettably the closing hole – a par-4 346-yard finish – is limited in its challenge and some cynics have been heard to describe Cypress Point somewhat unkindly as "the greatest seventeen-hole course in the world".

Cypress Point has hosted only one major event, the 1981 Walker Cup, but that should not be allowed to detract from its place in world golf as one of the most beautiful and spectacular spots to play the game.

California, USA

PGA West Palmer Course
La Quinta, California, USA

WITH five finishing holes artfully sculpted along the rugged Santa Rosa Mountains, Arnold Palmer has helped create a truly magnificent course worthy of tournament golf.

Host course to the PGA Tour's Humana Challenge, formerly known as the Bob Hope Classic, and sight of David Duval's 1999 win with a final round course record 59, the tournament boasts many big-name winners such as Mark Wilson in 2012, Bill Haas, in 2010, Phil Mickelson, in 2002 and 2004, Fred Couples, in 1998, Jack Nicklaus, in 1963, and Palmer himself winning a record five times, in 1960, 62, 68, 71 and 73.

From Hollywood's most high profile celebrities to US Presidents, the Palmer course has attracted a host of personalities drawn to the venue by its reputation.

The Palmer course is one of six offering 108 holes of championship golf and three clubhouses on a 2,000 acre complex and you don't have to be a member to play. Opened in 1987, the par 72 Palmer course was designed by Pete Dye with Palmer's input and is 6,931 yards long.

The 18th fairway features a plaque commemorating one of the most remarkable shots in PGA Tour history, when Duval hit his five iron to the green from 215 yards out setting up his eagle putt and a final round 59.

Mission Hills Country Club
Rancho Mirage, California, USA

MISSION HILLS COUNTRY CLUB, known worldwide for its history and tradition, is the home of the Dinah Shore Tournament Course and the sight for the first major in golf every year, the LPGA Kraft Nabisco Championship.

Designed in 1972 by Desmond Muirhead, the par 72 tournament course has hosted a major championship for more than 40 years.

The 18th is a 646 yard par-5 with an island green fronting the clubhouse. It invariably plays a significant role in determining the champion, including Brittany Lincicome's eagle in 2009 – the only time one of golf's majors was won on the final hole with an eagle.

Mission Hills has also hosted the PGA Club Professionals Championships, US Open qualifying and the US National Seniors.

Three courses form the complex. In addition to the 7,221 yard Dinah Shore Tournament Course, there are also the Arnold Palmer and Pete Dye Challenge courses, opened in 1979 and 1988 respectively.

Mission Hills also boasts 27 tennis courts and was the venue for the 1978 Davis Cup finals.

© Graeme Baxter

The Championships

Sam Snead pointing at the Opening Round Score, 1940.

CROWDER 5 OVER PAR

SNEAD 5 UNDER PAR

© Bettmann/Corbis

THERE is no record of when the term "major" was first used, but there is no doubt that the original major was the Open Championship, or as it is more commonly referred to "The Open."

There is no need to prefix Open with "British" as the world's oldest golf tournament played over 18 holes has a unique standing in the game.

First played in 1860 at Prestwick and won by Willie Park Senior from an entry of just eight players, the Open remains the tournament every leading professional wants most of all on his CV, given its history and tradition.

The first 12 stagings of the championship were at Prestwick before the Open moved to St Andrews in 1873. Today the rota consists of nine of Britain's finest links courses, but winning at the Old Course remains extra special as it is universally known as the home of golf.

The Claret Jug awarded to the Open champion is the most iconic trophy in golf and has been around since 1872.

Young Tom Morris, having earned the original Challenge Belt outright after winning the Open three years in a row, was the first to have his name engraved on the new trophy when he won again in 1872.

The second of the four majors, the US Open was first played in 1895 at Newport, Rhode Island and

won by an Englishman, Horace Rawlins on a nine-hole course.

At the time the US Open was considered secondary to the US Amateur Championship. But the following year the US Open moved to the 18-hole course at Shinnecock Hills, New York and quickly became established as second only to the Open in terms of its prestige.

The USPGA Championship was born in 1916 in the form of a matchplay tournament and remained so until 1957. It took some time for the third major to gain popularity but when the charismatic Walter Hagen began dominating the event in the 1920s, appearing in six out of seven consecutive finals and winning five of them, the USPGA became firmly established on the world stage.

Originally an invitational event and played for the first time in 1934, the Masters quickly acquired major status once it became open to qualifiers and is the only one of the four tournaments to be played at the same venue every year.

The Masters is now regarded as second only to the Open and Augusta's famous Green Jacket – first awarded to Sam Snead in 1949 – is one of the most coveted prizes in golf, almost but not quite as prized as the Claret Jug itself.

Jack Nicklaus with 18 has won more majors than anyone else and they are said to define a player's greatness. But there are those who argue that it is wrong to judge a player purely on the number of majors won.

Many of the game's finest players never won a major and Scotland's Colin Montgomerie is a case in point. Monty was a five-time runner-up and holds the record of being European number one eight times, including a remarkable seven years in a row.

In the four decades following the creation of the Open Championship, the number of golf tournaments with prize-money increased slowly. Most were in Britain and it was almost impossible for

British Open Championship at Prestwick, 1925.

the early professionals to earn a living from tournament golf, having to supplement their earnings with jobs as club pros.

But there was a steady increase in the number of championships in various countries of continental Europe and by the early years of the 20th Century France (1906), Belgium (1910), Germany (1911), Holland (1912) and Spain (1912) had established national Opens.

The European Masters came later, in 1923, while the Irish and Italian Opens were first contested in 1927.

While the majority of these championships have survived, the German Open was last held in 1999 and the Belgian equivalent 12 months later.

British players tended to dominate these events in the early years and they were represented by the Professional Golfers' Association, the forerunner of what became the PGA European Tour in 1972 and subsequently the European Tour.

By 1972 the season consisted of 20 tournaments, of which 12 were in the United Kingdom and one in Ireland. The remaining seven consisted of the Dutch, German, Italian, French, Madrid, Spanish and Swiss Opens.

In 1982 the tour expanded beyond Europe for the first time with the introduction of the Tunisian Open and by that year there were 27 tournaments. Two years later the European Tour became independent of the Professional Golfers' Association.

Very much alive to the risk of losing its best players to the PGA Tour in America, where the earnings potential is far greater, the European Tour introduced a bonus pool in 1988 with the aim of distributing extra prize-money at the end of the season to the most successful players.

That system continued for 10 years, after which renewed emphasis was placed on maximising prize-money in individual tournaments.

By then the European Tour had become global with the creation of the Dubai Desert Classic in 1989, the first tournament to be staged in Asia. Three years later the Johnnie Walker Classic came into being in Bangkok.

A short time later the European Tour launched a policy of co-sanctioning tournaments with other PGA Tours, most notably South Africa and Australasia while also expanding its wings in Asia.

Today the European Tour is truly global and it is second only to the PGA Tour in terms of finance and prestige.

The rise of the Swedes as a major force in the game and the emergence of outstanding players from France, Germany, Italy and Spain in the footsteps of Seve Ballesteros – the man who revolutionised European golf in the late 1970s and 1980s – and the remarkable run of success achieved by Irish players has strengthened European golf to the extent that a number of American players regularly compete in Europe.

There have even been calls for the European Tour's flagship event, the BMW PGA Championship to be recognised as the fifth major, in the same way that the Players Championship at Sawgrass has been similarly touted.

In a further attempt to strengthen the European Tour, the Order of Merit was replaced by the Race to Dubai in 2009, culminating in the Dubai World

A proud Tony Jacklin holding the Open trophy in 1969.

© Hulton-Deutsch Collection/Corbis

Championship, with a bonus pool of $7.5million distributed among the top 15 players at the end of the season, in addition to a prize-pot of £7.5million in Dubai.

By a cruel twist of fate, the announcement coincided with a global economic downturn, resulting in an immediate reduction in funds.

This was followed by subsequent further reductions.

The leading 60 European players contest the end-of-season event, which is now part of "The Final Series" of four tournaments, including the BMW Masters, the WGC-HSBC Champions and the Turkish Airlines Open.

It is a measure of the growth of the game in Asia and emergence of China on the international golf scene and that vast country's influence that it now hosts the Volvo China Open, the BMW Masters and the WGC-HSBC Champions.

The explosion in prize-money has also been phenomenal. In 1972, the total worth of the 19 events in Europe was £266,867. By 2013 that figure had mushroomed to a staggering £111,562,068, covering 46 tournaments.

South African Ernie Els is the leading all-time European Tour money-winner at the time of publication, having amassed £29,467,156 in prize-money to the end of the 2013 season.

Former Ryder Cup-winning captain Sam Torrance holds the record for most events played and finishes in the money, 704 and 509, while Colin Montgomerie has achieved most top ten finishes, 184.

Monty also shares the record of six tournament victories in a season, along with Seve Ballesteros, Sir Nick Faldo and Lee Westwood.

But the late Ballesteros remains out in front with most official European Tour International scheduled victories. His total of 50 is eight more than Bernhard Langer has achieved.

The global nature of the European Tour is highlighted by the international schedule of 47 tournaments in 26 countries.

Four of the first five tournaments of the 2014 season were played in South Africa with a visit to Hong Kong in between prior to the Middle East swing in Abu Dhabi, Qatar and Dubai.

Following a return to South Africa for a further three tournaments, Morocco, Malaysia, China and South Korea featured on the schedule before the main focus switched to Europe in May through to September.

The European Tour, which is based at the Wentworth Club in Virginia Water, Surrey, also operates the Seniors Tour and the Challenge Tour.

The American tour began in 1929 and underwent several name changes before eventually becoming the PGA Tour in 1975.

But it is not the governing body of golf in America. Instead, that is the responsibility of the United States Golf Association, which organises the US Open.

What the PGA Tour does is organise the week-to-week events. It also runs the main tournaments on five other tours, including The Champions Tour for over 50s, the PGA Tour Canada and PGA Tour China.

The introduction of the FedEx Cup in 2005 and first awarded two

Manette Le Blan winning the Womens Open Golf Championship in 1928.

© Hulton-Deutsch Collection/Corbis

years later was a major innovation on the PGA Tour, leading to a revamp of the tournament schedule.

From January through to mid-August players compete in regular events and earn FedEx Cup points, in addition to prize-money. Then at the end of the regular season, the top 125 FedEx Cup points winners compete in the play-off series of four events, with the field sizes reduced to 100 to 70 and finally 30 for the Tour Championship.

The Tour Championship is preceded by the Barclays Classic, the Deutsche Bank Championship and the BMW Championship, in turn.

The cash-rich World Golf Championship (WGC) events are co-sanctioned by the International Federation of PGA Tours and are for the leading golfers worldwide.

Among the best known PGA Tournaments are the Arnold Palmer Invitational, the Memorial Tournament – founded by Jack Nicklaus – the AT&T National – hosted by Tiger Woods – the Hyundai Tournament of Champions, the Honda Classic, the Greenbrier Classic, the Sony Open and the RBC Heritage.

While the late Sam Snead holds the record of most titles with 82 victories it will come as no surprise to learn that Tiger Woods stands alone as the biggest money-earner in PGA history.

Woods, leading money-winner 10 times and PGA player of the Year a remarkable 11 times, had banked a staggering $109,504,139 as of the 2013 season – $36million more than his closest rival, Phil Mickelson.

The Champions Tour and the European Senior Tour compete for five majors: The Senior PGA Championship, The Tradition, Senior Players Championship, US Senior Open and Senior British Open.

Women's golf also has five majors: The Kraft Nabisco Championship, the LPGA Championship, the US Women's Open, the Women's British Open and the Evian Championship. ■

Ode to Golf

In my hand I hold a ball,
White and dimpled, and rather
small.
Oh, how bland it does appear,
This harmless looking little sphere.
By its size I could not guess,
Or the awesome strength it does
possess.
But since I fell beneath its spell,
I've wandered through the fires of
Hell,
My life has not been quite the
same,
Since I chose to play this stupid
game.
It rules my mind for hours on end,
A fortune it has made me spend.
It has made me curse and made
me cry,
And hate myself and want to die.
It promises me a thing called Par,
If I hit it straight and far.
To master such a tiny ball,
Should not be very hard at all.
But my desires the ball refuses,
And does exactly as it chooses.
It hooks and slices, dribbles and
dies,
And disappears before my eyes.
Often it will have a whim,
To hit a tree or take a swim.
With miles of grass on which to
land,
It finds a tiny patch of sand.
Then has me offering up my soul,
If only it would find the hole:
It's made me whimper like a pup,
And swear that I will give it up.
And take to drink to ease my
sorrow,
But the ball knows...I'll be back
tomorrow.

– Anon.

Old Tom Morris

SELECTING just ten from the thousands of professional golfers who have graced the game over the years is a daunting task.

How do you separate the great from the good? What criteria do you apply to determine true greatness in a sport which has produced so many outstanding champions?

But there are undoubtedly those whose influence on the game has been enormous, starting with the man generally regarded as the first true professional and the game's founding father, OLD TOM MORRIS.

Born in St Andrews on 16 June 1821, Morris went on to revolutionise golf as a player, club-maker, administrator, innovator, course designer and father figure.

He won the Open Championship four times – in 1861, '62, '64 and '67 – and remains the oldest winner of the world's first major championship, having triumphed at Prestwick in 1867 at the age of 46 years and 99 days.

Having started playing the game at the age of six, Morris was apprenticed as a ball-maker for Allan Robertson, his senior by six years and a prolific winner of money matches as the best player of his age.

Robertson and Morris were unbeaten at foursomes. Yet, the latter was by no means perfect, his one flaw being his putting and his habit of missing from close range. Indeed in modern terminology he appears to have suffered from the "yips."

But Old Tom's weakness on the green did not prevent him from carving out a reputation as a formidable rival.

He went to Prestwick in 1851 as Keeper of the Green and established the course that hosted the first 12 Opens, finishing runner-up to Musselburgh's Willie Park in the inaugural championship.

Morris' successful defence in 1862 by a remarkable 13 strokes was a record in the major championships that stood until 2000 when Tiger Woods won the US Open by 15.

He returned to his home town as Keeper of the Green on the Old Course where he was paid the princely sum of £50 a year by the R&A. It is testimony to his skills as a course designer that the course we know today essentially evolved under his care.

In addition to laying out Prestwick's original 12 hole track, Old Tom was also influential in creating the masterpieces that are St Andrews New, Carnoustie, Dornoch and Muirfield, among many.

A deeply religious man who established the convention that the Old Course should not be played on a Sunday, he is also said to have influenced many of the finest course architects who came later.

Tom Morris senior, British golfer, portrait, c1910.

© Heritage Images/Corbis

Morris remained at St Andrews until his death in May 1908 at the age of 86, as the result of a fall down the stairs of the New Club, where he regularly held court in his later years.

What Morris' son Young Tom would have gone on to achieve is impossible to say, given that he died at the age of just 24 in December 1875.

The younger Morris had by then matched his father's feat in winning four Opens and remains the youngest champion, at the age of 17 years, five months and eight days following his success in 1868, the first of four consecutive victories – the only player to do so.

It is said that Young Tom first started hitting balls on the beach at Prestwick not long after he had learned to walk and newspaper reports of the time described his style as the only model for a first class player.

His short life came to a tragic end when his wife and baby died in childbirth, leading him to suffer depression and problems with alcohol.

He was found dead in bed on Christmas morning, having apparently suffered a ruptured artery that bled into his lung. But there were those romantics who insisted that he had died of a broken heart.

Old and Young Tom Morris.

Harry Vardon

THEY were golf's so-called "Great Triumvirate" of Vardon, Taylor and Braid who between them won 16 Opens and dominated the game around the turn of the 20th Century.

Born within a year of each other, the trio were virtually untouchable for a 21 year period between 1894 and 1914.

But it was Jersey-born HARRY VARDON who perhaps achieved the greatest fame as the only man to win the Open six times while JH (John Henry) Taylor, from Devon, and Scot James Braid, who hailed from the Fife village of Earlsferry, secured five victories apiece.

Vardon remains a prominent figure to this day as the silhouette on the European Tour's official logo. Two trophies also bear his name: The European Tour's order of merit title and for the stroke average title in America.

He was regarded as the finest player of his generation, with one estimate suggesting that at one stage he won 17 tournaments out of 22 and finished runner-up in the other five.

The remarkable Channel Islander also finished first, second and second in three appearances in the US Open over the course of 20 years, winning the second oldest major in 1900.

Given that golf was not then the international game it has subsequently become, Vardon's willingness to cross the Atlantic helped popularise golf.

He was also involved in one of the game's biggest upsets when a previously unheard of 20-year-old amateur, Francis Quimet beat him and Englishman Ted Ray in a play-off for the US Open title in 1913.

He began as a caddie at Grouville, near St Helier and quickly developed a natural bent for the game although his father claimed that Vardon's brother Tom was a more accomplished player.

His first Open win came at Muirfield in 1896 after a play-off against Taylor; his last in 1914, at Prestwick, where Taylor again finished second.

The second half of his career was afflicted by ill health after he was diagnosed with tuberculosis. But his health problems also turned out to be a stroke of good fortune when he was forced to cancel a trip to America in 1912, having been booked to sail on the ill-fated Titanic.

Slimly built, Vardon was blessed with an elegant and easy upright style of swing in contrast to the "St Andrews swing", where the club was swept round the body. He also popularised the overlapping grip.

Vardon, who was also the professional at South Herts for many years, designed a number of courses prior to his death in March 1937 at the age of 66.

Taylor learned his game at Westward Ho where

Harry Vardon popularised the overlapping grip.

he was both a caddie and a greenkeeper and was credited with being a master in the wind due to his traditional flat swing.

Already in possession of two Open titles before Vardon won his first, Taylor was a runner-up no fewer than six times. But his most satisfying achievement was winning at St Andrews in 1900, when he produced the lowest score in every round to win by eight shots from Vardon.

He became the professional at Royal Mid Surrey, one of the many courses he designed, and was instrumental in setting up the Professional Golfers' Association. He died in February 1963, aged 91, having also captained the Gt. Britain Ryder Cup team 30 years earlier.

Tall and powerful, Braid possessed a fine short game to compensate for his occasional waywardness off the tee and was a flamboyant and exciting player to watch.

His five Open victories were achieved in a period of 10 years between 1901 and 1910 and he was runner-up on a further four occasions.

Braid, who lived until the age of 80, dying in November 1950, became the first professional at Walton Heath, Surrey and is credited with several outstanding course designs including the Kings and Queens at Gleneagles.

The noted golf writer Bernard Darwin described the "Great Triumvirate" thus: "Vardon played as if he was enjoying the game, Braid as if he were going through his day's work, and Taylor, in certain moods at any rate, as if he hated it."

Bobby Jones

NO player can ever be defined as the greatest to have played the game, but BOBBY JONES was unquestionably one of the very best and most popular.

Christened Robert Tyre Jones, the golfer who became known as "The Emperor" achieved the "Grand Slam" in 1930 to confirm his status as the most successful amateur player to grace the game.

He began by sealing victory in the British Amateur Championship with a 7&6 victory over Roger Wethered and followed it up with his third Open Championship – at Hoylake – before sinking a 40 foot putt on the final green to win the US Open at Interlachen by two shots from Macdonald Smith.

That left only the US Amateur at Merion, where Jones strode to a majestic 8&7 triumph over Eugene Homans in the final.

But instead of building further on his remarkable successes, Jones chose to announce his retirement from the game at few months later at the age of just 28.

He had by then won a staggering 13 of the 21 national championships he had entered in just eight seasons while the two men regarded as the greatest professionals of their generation, Walter Hagen and Gene Sarazen never won when Jones was in the field.

Jones' final count was four US Opens, five US Amateur, three Open and one Amateur Championship titles.

Born in 1902 in Atlanta, Jones had a remarkably strong mindset and an exquisite, truly graceful swing. He also refused at all times to play safe, claiming that he was driven to play every shot with all his worth.

Yet, for all that he was a quiet and unassuming man perceived as gentle, intelligent and charming by his millions of fans, Jones also had an explosive temper which he found difficult to control at times, leading to several verbal outbursts and club-throwing incidents that incurred the threat of a ban by the US Golf Association on one occasion. He was also prone to nerves and anxiety.

What more he might have achieved had he

Bobby Jones – Open Championship at St. Andrews, July 9th 1927.

© Hulton-Deutsch Collection/Corbis

chosen to extend his career and join the professional ranks is impossible to say, but few sportsmen have been honoured by not one but two tickertape parades through the streets of New York.

With degrees in engineering, literature and law from Georgia Tech and Harvard, Jones went into business and the law on his retirement and became a highly successful businessman. He also created Augusta National and set up the Masters in 1934.

He enlisted for military service during World War II, becoming an officer in the Army Air Corp and later served overseas.

It was a measure of his popularity that when he stopped off at St Andrews in 1936 to play the Old Course – scene of his Open triumph nine years earlier - en route to the Berlin Olympics 5,000 people turned out to watch "Oor Bobby."

He later became only the second American after Benjamin Franklin to be given the Freedom of the Royal Burgh of St Andrews in 1958, by which time his health was in steady decline.

Regrettably, Jones spent the final 20 years of his life largely incapacitated by a disease of the spinal column before passing away at the age of 69 in December 1971.

Even with the immaculate Jones prominent on the scene, Hagen, who lived to the age of 76, and Sarazen, who was 97, enjoyed considerable success.

Rochester-born Hagen, seen as golf's first great showman with his colourful outfits and almost arrogant air that earned him the moniker "Sir Walter", captured 11 major titles and played in five Ryder Cup matches.

Fellow New Yorker Sarazen, who was of Italian descent, for his part achieved 41 career victories including seven majors and was the first player to win all four majors.

He also invented the sand-wedge and was an honorary starter at Augusta until shortly before his death in 1999.

> Golf is a game whose aim is to hit a very small ball into an even smaller hole, with weapons singularly ill-designed for the purpose –
>
> *Winston Churchill*

GOLF QUIP

Ben Hogan

Ben Hogan holds the PGA Trophy he won at the Norwood Hills Country Club Tourney. He beat Mike Turnesa in the final round to win the coveted cup.

BEN HOGAN did not suffer fools gladly. Reportedly unapproachable, Hogan appears to have been a complex man who aspired to achieve perfection on the golf course and in life.

It must also be said that he was one of the finest golfers of all time and, according to many of his contemporaries, the greatest ever shot-maker.

If, as appears to have been the case, Hogan was the "Wee Ice Man" it is perhaps not all that surprising, given that few things in life came easy to him.

At the age of only nine he had to deal with the death of his father, who committed suicide by shooting himself.

Born in Fort Worth in August 1912, he came up through the caddie ranks before turning pro in 1929 and struggled at first, finding himself broke several times and forced to do odd jobs in the winter, including working as a croupier.

It in fact took Hogan until 1940 to win the first of his 64 PGA Tour titles, the North and South Open. But after that there was no stopping the 5' 7" Texan with the steely resolve and the capacity to overcome a natural violent hook that had hampered his progress in the early years of his career.

He was the leading PGA Tour money winner in 1940, '41 and '42 before losing three years to military service and also in 1946 and again in '48.

After also winning the Vardon Trophy for the lowest stroke average in 1940, '41 and '48, when he was also named PGA Player of the Year, Hogan was once again the victim of misfortune.

In February 1949, while driving along a road in Texas, Hogan's car ran into a Greyhound bus that was overtaking a truck, and at the moment of impact he threw himself across the front seat to protect his wife, Valerie, saving both her life and his.

But Hogan suffered a broken collar bone and

Ben Hogan seated on the back of a car in the homecoming parade on Broadway in 1953.

fractures to hip, ribs, pelvis and ankle. A blood clot also developed and almost killed him.

It was a year before he could play, but he never had normal circulation in his legs again.

For a time doctors feared he might not walk, let alone play golf.

But not only did Hogan recover sufficiently to return to competitive golf, he went on to achieve even greater successes.

A movie was made in 1951 charting Hogan's astonishing comeback, "Follow the Sun" starring Glenn Ford in the principal role.

But not even Hollywood would have dared come up with the true life script that Hogan penned in the wake of his brush with death.

Having already won USPGA twice and the US Open prior to his accident, he went on to collect six more majors.

He won the US Open three more times, the Masters twice and the Open. But the most remarkable of these triumphs was his 1950 US Open victory at Merion months after his comeback.

Then in 1953 he triumphed at Carnoustie in addition to winning the Masters and the US Open, playing in just six tournaments and winning five of them.

The wee man in the white cap was a true inspiration for all of those challenging adversity and undoubtedly one of the true greats of the game.

In spite of the horrific injuries he suffered, Hogan was just one month short of his 85th birthday when he died in 1997.

Hogan was part of an outstanding trio that included fellow Americans Byron Nelson - a near neighbour and close rival in the local caddies' championship - and Sam Snead, all born within six months of each other.

Nelson, who lived to the grand age of 94, had a relatively short career, retiring in his mid-30s, but achieved much, including an astonishing run of 11 consecutive victories in 1945.

In his 14 years as a pro he also captured five majors, the Masters and the USPGA Championship, each twice, and the US Open.

On retiring Nelson became a cattle rancher in his native Texas and a television commentator.

Virginian Snead, meanwhile, was known as "Slammin' Sam" because of his prowess as a long hitter. He also possessed the balance, rhythm and timing to collect 165 titles, seven of which were majors.

Like Nelson the three-time Ryder Cup captain enjoyed longevity, passing away just four days short of his 90th birthday in 2002.

Arnold Palmer

HE was the first of golf's superstars in the television age; a working-class hero who had his own army of fans on both sides of the Atlantic.

ARNOLD PALMER was the son of a greenkeeper and professional at Latrobe on the outskirts of industrial Pittsburgh and he was brought up the hard way after having a golf club thrust into his tiny hands at the age of just three and being advised to, "Just hit it as hard as you can and then go and find the ball."

It can be argued that he spent the rest of his life doing exactly that although he was not without natural skill to compliment his raw power.

After completing military service in the Coast Guard, Palmer won the US Amateur in 1954 at the age of 24, turning pro a short time later.

He claimed his maiden professional victory the following year when he won the Canadian Open, the first of 95 tour successes, later adding 10 senior titles to his hugely impressive tally.

But it was three years later that Palmer really arrived on the scene, winning the first of four Green Jackets at the 1958 Masters and "Arnie's Army" was born.

He also went on to win the US Open in 1960 and back-to-back Opens in 1961 and '62, securing his seven major triumphs within a span of just six years.

Palmer would undoubtedly have won many more but for the arrival on the scene of his great rival Jack Nicklaus in 1961.

But despite many subsequent disappointments, Palmer remained hugely popular with his adoring fans and millions more watching on TV who loved his cavalier style and charismatic personality.

Aware of the benefits to be derived from television broadcasting golf, Palmer embraced the medium and used it to his advantage by playing to the galleries and the cameras.

And he was still the darling of the crowd at the age of 65 when he walked up the 18th at the Old Course in 1995 as he bid farewell to the Open to rapturous applause.

Nowadays this man of the people oversees a

Arnold Palmer, April 1956.

© Jerry Cooke/Corbis

business empire that has grown over the years into a multi-million dollar concern after setting new records as an aviator.

In 1976, he flew around the world in 58 hours in a Learjet and 20 years later bought his first Cessna Citation and promptly set a speed record over a 3,000 mile course.

Perhaps the biggest compliment paid to Palmer came from Nicklaus, who said of his great rival: "There has never been anyone like him before in the game and there probably won't be another like him again."

Born in the same year as Palmer, Peter Thomson eclipsed Arnie's Open record, becoming one of only a handful of players to raise the Claret Jug five times.

The 84-year-old Australian, who spends part of the year living in his beloved St Andrews, arrived in Britain from his native Melbourne in the early 1950s and established a remarkable record in the oldest major.

In addition to winning in successive years from 1954 to 1956, Thomson made it five victories when he also triumphed in 1958 and 1965.

Moreover, from his debut in 1951 to '71 he was only out of the top-nine three times, and in seven Opens from 1952 he finished second, second, first, first, first, second, first. He was also the only player in the 20th Century to claim a hat-trick of titles.

But the multi-talented sportsman, journalist, author, commentator and course designer surprisingly never managed to crack the American scene, winning only once in the States.

Arnold Palmer is shown holding his head as he kneels on the 3rd green, after missing his putt, during the 97th Open at Carnoustie in 1968.

© Bettmann/Corbis

Gary Player

Player competes in the 1987 Open, East Lothian, dressed in his trademark black outfit.

P ART of the "Big Three" with Palmer and Jack Nicklaus, GARY PLAYER was the first truly international golfer.

The diminutive and slight South African left his homeland in the mid-1950s, first to compete in Britain and later to challenge the might of American golf in a way that no others from outside the States had managed to do with such success.

Countryman Bobby Locke had blazed a trail of sorts with his four Open wins, but Player became a global star, clocking up millions of air miles in pursuit of the game's greatest prizes.

Even today, seven decades on, the remarkable 78-year-old remains a leading figure in the world of golf, promoting the game's cause worldwide.

But Player's fame does not derive from just his golfing exploits. Always outspoken, he has also influenced politics and politicians and in 2000 was named among the top five of his nation's most influential people in addition to being voted South Africa's greatest ever athlete.

Tough, feisty, courageous, Player is a man with strong principals while also also blessed with that rare ability to freely admit to his mistakes.

Once a supporter of apartheid, he later had the courage to denounce it and went as far as to name the late Nelson Mandela as his hero.

Prior to that Player had been subjected to threats and intimidation by anti-apartheid activists who attacked him both verbally and physically on the golf course.

But golf's Little Big Man stood up to his many detractors and overcame adversity in a way that few others would have managed to do.

When he first left South Africa in 1955, he was dismissively told by his British peers that he might be better advised to return to Johannesburg and find a more suitable occupation.

He did so, but not with his tail between his legs. Aware that his hookers grip and flat swing needed much work, he grafted with such tenacity to improve it and other aspects of his game that he was crowned South African Open champion just a year later – the first of 13 national titles.

Encouraged by his success, Player returned once more to Britain and won the Dunlop tournament before deciding to try his luck on the PGA Tour.

The rest, as they say, is history. The man dubbed the "Black Knight" because of his habit of invariably dressing from head to foot in black clothing won the first of his nine majors – more than any other player born outside the US - in 1959, becoming Open champion at the age of just 23.

Two years later he became the first non-American to win the Masters at Augusta and in 1962 won the first of his two USPGA titles.

When Player then added the US Open to his burgeoning collection in 1965 he became only the third player to win all four majors after Gene Sarazen and Ben Hogan prior to Jack Nicklaus and Tiger Woods joining the elite club.

He enjoyed further Masters success in 1974 and '78 and when he won the Open for a third time in 1974 to add to his triumphs at Muirfield in '59 and Carnoustie in '68 he became the only golfer of the 20th Century to raise the Claret Jug aloft in three different decades.

Player also captured five World Match Play titles in a glittering career that saw him win 163 times on tour, including nine senior majors.

Not the most naturally gifted, Player has always been keen to emphasise the importance of a strict physical fitness regime and a sound diet.

He also famously declared, "The more I practice, the luckier I get" in reference to his phenomenal work ethic.

Although a tireless worker in his efforts to enact political change and a keen supporter of the underprivileged in his homeland, setting up a foundation to educate deprived children, Player has not always been popular with his fellow professionals.

Some take umbrage at his fiercely held views on a myriad of subjects ranging from religion to lifestyle and his tendency to preach his message. But few would question Gary Player's standing in the game he has graced for 60 years.

Jack Nicklaus

THE facts speak for themselves. JACK NICKLAUS is the most successful golfer on the planet and appears increasingly likely to remain so for the foreseeable future.

Only Tiger Woods poses a threat to the "Golden Bear's" record of 18 major championship wins. But whereas Woods appeared nailed on to surpass Nicklaus' total, that is no longer the case.

The game's most prolific winner of majors may not have enjoyed the same level of popularity as Arnold Palmer, or been blessed with the charisma of another of his great rivals, Lee Trevino, but he was nonetheless admired as a gracious player and a fierce competitor.

Nicklaus' refusal to ever give up is highlighted by a remarkable statistic. During a run of 154 consecutive majors, he finished in the top-10 in half of them and was runner-up a staggering 19 times.

His longevity as a contender was also quite astonishing. He won the first of his majors – the US Open – in 1962 and the last of them – the Masters – in 1986, a time span of 24 years.

In between he collected three Open titles, three US Opens, five USPGA championships and five Green Jackets.

Born in Columbus, Ohio in January 1940, Nicklaus was introduced to golf by his father Charlie at the local country club and by the age of 16 had won the Ohio State Open.

Taught the finer points of the game by Jack Grout, who had grown up in Texas playing with Ben Hogan and Byron Nelson, Nicklaus was powerful off the tee, hit magnificent iron shots and putted consistently well.

He was perhaps not the most naturally gifted player, but his course management was better than anyone else's and he was blessed with a powerful mindset.

It was also said that Nicklaus often plotted his way round the course in a deliberately slower pace than necessary in the knowledge that by doing so he would play his own game for longer than his opponent and also increase the pressure on his nearest challengers.

Having won the US Amateur twice, Nicklaus' first victory as a professional was the US Open in 1962, defeating Arnold Palmer in a play-off in his rival's home state of Pennsylvania at Oakmont.

With a crew cut and on the chubby side, Nicklaus was abused by a section of the gallery for having the temerity to beat their hero, but it was a measure of his mental strength that he did not allow the taunts to affect him.

In 1966 Nicklaus became the first player to win successive Masters titles and in the same year he also won the Open at Muirfield, later naming his own course in Ohio "Muirfield Village" in recognition of his first success in Britain.

Jack Nicklaus at the Open, St Andrews, in 1978.

© Leo Mason/Corbis

His Open win gave him the first of three sets of Grand Slam titles. But winning the Open twice at St Andrews probably meant more to Nicklaus than any of his other 112 victories, given that it is home of golf.

However, it was his record sixth win at Augusta at the age of 46 that was the most remarkable of all, coming as it did in his 25th year as a pro.

Twelve years later, 21 months short of his 60th birthday, he achieved another notable milestone at Augusta when he became the oldest player to achieve a top-10 finish at a major, a record that would later be broken by his old sparring partner Tom Watson.

Nicklaus' sportsmanship was never more clearly demonstrated than at the Ryder Cup in 1969 when he conceded a short but missable putt to Tony Jacklin to tie the overall match, explaining: "I don't think you would have missed that putt but under the circumstances I would never give you the opportunity."

Given his talents and longevity Nicklaus might have been expected to have won even more, but he was always careful to pace himself, playing relatively few tournaments to ensure he remained fresh as well as spending time with his family.

He was also in competition with a golden generation featuring the likes of Palmer, Lee Trevino, Watson, Player, Raymond Floyd, Johnny Miller and Hale Irwin, winners of a combined total of 39 major championships.

Tom Watson

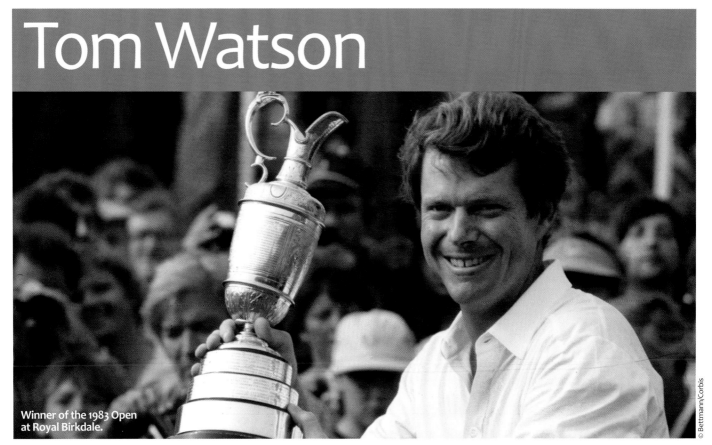

Winner of the 1983 Open at Royal Birkdale.

On a warm July afternoon in 2009 TOM WATSON came within eight feet of arguably the greatest sporting achievement of all time.

At the age of 59 and long past his peak, the five-time Open champion stood on the 18th green at Turnberry on the cusp of golfing immortality.

Not even the most fanciful Hollywood scriptwriter would dare to have penned the script for such a drama, but there was to be a sickening, gut-wrenching twist in the tail.

With the adrenalin pumping through his body Watson sent his approach shot over the green and in the space of a minute or so he suddenly became his age again as he faced a putt to equal Harry Vardon's record of six Open wins and make the headline writers' dreams come true.

History records that fellow American Stewart Cink won the play-off to muted applause without having to break sweat. But those of us who witnessed the drama instinctively knew he would.

As Watson himself said, it would have been a hell of a story. Instead the atmosphere bordered on funereal.

How different from another sunny July afternoon on the Ayrshire coast 32 years earlier when Watson and Jack Nicklaus staged one of the most absorbing head-to-heads of all time. On that occasion Watson won his Duel in the Sun.

No doubt that week he also fed off the memories of 1977 at the golf course that has become synonymous with his name.

But no matter that he later admitted that the moment the romantic dream died tore at his gut on a regular basis, he somehow managed to conduct himself with the dignity of a truly great champion during the post-championship media conference.

With hardened journalists and commentators almost scared to break the deafening silence, some close to inconsolable, Watson quipped: "What's up, guys? This aint a funeral, you know."

It was not a moment for laughter, but at least we were allowed to smile briefly and marvel at the fortitude of the man. Other, lesser mortals would have sought the solitude of a darkened room and locked themselves away for days, refusing all contact with the outside world.

A true gentleman and a keen historian of the game, Watson has always possessed an inner strength and the mental toughness required to win eight major championships in as many years, making him the game's best player in the mid to late 1970s and early '80s.

Born in Kansas City in September 1949, Watson turned pro in 1971 after graduating from Stanford University, having been introduced to the game by his father.

He was no great shakes initially, but with the help of Byron Nelson his game quickly developed and by 1975 it was good enough to earn him his first major, the Open Championship at Carnoustie, where he defeated Australian Jack Newton in an 18-hole play-off.

Three more victories followed on Scottish links courses, at Turnberry, in 1977, Muirfield, in 1980, and Troon, in '82, before Watson added Royal Birkdale to his list of conquests the following year.

Yet, incredibly he had hated links golf at first, only learning to love that form of golf after the third of his Open wins once he had eventually come to terms with the unpredictable bounce of the ball!

He was also Masters champion in 1977 and '81 and winner of the US Open in '82. In addition he won the Senior British Open three times.

The leading PGA Tour money winner for four years in a row from 1977, Watson also regularly beat Nicklaus when he was at his peak, but he was never quite the same player again after losing out to Seve Ballesteros in the 1984 Open at St Andrews after he went over the green at the 17th and ended up against a stone wall.

His putting stroke deserted him for several years, but he eventually rediscovered some of his old magic and remained capable of winning on the PGA Tour into his late 40s.

Still a force on the Champions Tour, Watson captained the United States to victory in the 1993 Ryder Cup and was re-appointed to the role for the 2014 match at Gleneagles.

Severiano Ballesteros

HE was probably the most loved golfer ever. SEVERIANO BALLESTEROS was also the best thing that ever happened to European golf, re-popularising the game across the Continent and taking it to a new level.

Handsome, dashing, passionate, immensely talented, often unconventional, a sometimes occasional outrageous risk-taker, confrontational and prone to dark moods, charismatic, cheeky and mischievous at the same time with a natural wit and an accent that almost mimicked the character of Manuel in Fawlty Towers, to the delight of his adoring public, Seve appealed to all ages across the sporting spectrum.

The swashbuckling Spanish matador of the fairways captured five major titles, but it would be wrong to measure Seve's career purely in the number of championships won, for he was much more than just a ferocious competitor.

The leader of golf's so-called "Famous Five", which included Sandy Lyle, Bernhard Langer, Ian Woosnam and Nick Faldo, Seve was wild and brilliant by turns, but he was never mundane or ordinary.

It was a measure of the esteem and affection in which he was held that when he died at the age of just 54 on May 7, 2011, his passing was greeted by a collective sense of sadness around the world.

Seve had long ceased to be a contender when he was diagnosed with a brain tumour in the autumn of 2008 after collapsing at Madrid airport. His back

The Spanish golf legend in action during a golf tournament at Santona, northern Spain.

© Victor Fraile/Corbis

was already an issue as a consequence of the stress he had put on it the way he drove the ball with such power and force by the time he won the last of his majors, the Open at Royal Lytham in 1988.

It was the third of his Open titles after he had also been crowned champion at the same venue in 1979 and at St Andrews five years later when the photograph of him fist-pumping on the 18th green became one of the most iconic images in golf.

He also had two green jackets following his Masters triumphs in 1980 and '83. But, in truth, he was never a lover of America or Americans and that was a driving force for his exploits in the Ryder Cup.

Having lost on his first two appearances in the biennial match, in 1979 and '83, Seve instilled a belief in his team-mates that the Americans could be beaten and they duly won in '85 and 87' before drawing the '89 match to retain the trophy as holders.

Two further losses followed before Europe again triumphed in 1995. But his proudest moment came two years later when he captained the hosts to a 14½-13½ victory on Spanish soil at Valderrama.

Born at the small fishing village of Pedrena, near Santander in northern Spain on April 9, 1957, Seve was the youngest of five brothers. Money was tight when he was growing up and he spent much of his early days playing with a 3-iron on the nearby beach. It was here that he learned the art of improvisation.

His uncle, Ramon Sota was already the country's most famous player when Seve turned pro in 1974, but within two years he was challenging his relation's status when he won the first of his 50 European Tour titles, the Dutch Open.

He subsequently went on to win 94 times worldwide, including nine victories on the PGA Tour. He was also Europe's leading money-winner six times and was voted European Player of the Century in 2000 before announcing his retirement on the eve of the 2007 Open at Carnoustie.

By then the Seve Trophy had been firmly established. The event was begun in 2000 to celebrate his love of international team match play golf.

But perhaps the tribute that best summed up Seve was delivered by Tiger Woods. "He was probably the most creative player who has ever played the game," declared Tiger. "He was a genius."

It was a mark of that genius that Seve's career paralleled those of Lyle, Langer, Woosnam and Faldo, in Europe, the American trio of Curtis Strange, Ben Crenshaw and Payne Stewart, Australian Greg Norman and Zimbabwe's Nick Price. Collectively they won 23 majors.

Yet, only Faldo surpassed Seve's tally, winning three Opens and three Green Jackets. But in spite of laying claim to being Britain's greatest ever player, Faldo – later Knighted for his services to golf – has never been loved in the same way Seve was.

The Open Championship 1984.

© Tony Roberts/Corbis

Tiger Woods

THE golf world had never seen anyone quite like him. When ELDRICK "TIGER" WOODS erupted on the world scene in 1996 at the age of 20 he was already a three-time US Amateur champion in successive years, having become the first person to also win three US Junior Amateur titles.

He could not possibly replicate that success in the paid ranks, or could he? The answer was delivered in Tiger's fifth tournament as a professional when he won the Las Vegas Invitational, beating Davis Love III in a play-off.

He won again from only eight starts and became the Rookie of the Year to confirm his glittering potential. The kid from Cypress, California was indeed a very special talent.

It is claimed that Tiger was still a baby when, having watched his father Earl swinging a club, he decided to have a go himself. What is fact is that by the age of two he was putting with Bob Hope on a TV show.

At three he won a pitch-and-putt competition for 10-year-olds, and he was playing off scratch by the time he was 13. The driving force behind the child prodigy was his father who oversaw every aspect of his son's golfing education.

Given the name "Tiger" by his father, a lieutenant in the Green Berets who served two terms in Vietnam, after a colleague who had saved his life and who later died at the hands of the Vietcong, the young cub showed his claws early, playing in four PGA events at the age of just 16.

Three years later, in 1995, the Stanford University graduate played in his first majors, making the cut in the Masters and the Open Championship.

Displaying the remarkable powers of concentration and mental resilience that have hallmarked his remarkable career, Tiger was soon out-thinking his opponents to the extent that he was a major champion within a year of turning pro.

The first of his 14 major successes arrived at Augusta in April 1997, where he posted the lowest-ever four-round total, beating Tom Kite into second by a staggering 12 strokes.

But there was even better to come in the summer of 2000 when he produced arguably the best golf of his career to win the US Open by 15 strokes and the Open a month later at St Andrews by eight, prompting Jack Nicklaus to comment: "When he gets ahead, I think he is superior to me. I never spread-eagled the field."

In winning the Open, Tiger became the youngest player to complete the Grand Slam of majors and only the fifth ever to do so. Then the following April, with his second Masters victory, he became the first person to hold all four major championships at the same time.

Tiger successfully defended his Masters title 12 months later before claiming a fourth Green Jacket in 2005, the same year that he held the Claret Jug aloft for a second time, again at St Andrews.

US Open champion in 2002 and '08 and winner of the USPGA Championship in 1999, 2002, '06 and '07, Tiger again showed his tremendous resolve when he defended his Open title at Hoylake in July 2006, just two months after the death of his father, and produced a sublime display of iron play on the baked-hard Liverpool links.

It appeared at that stage that it was only a matter of time before Nicklaus' record was broken, but the 2008 US Open brought his run to at least a temporary halt, albeit his victory at Torrey pines was all the more remarkable, given that he played with a broken leg and against doctors' orders.

Since then, Tiger, whose Achilles heel as a player has been the Ryder Cup, where he has struggled to fit into the team environment, has undergone a series of operations on his left knee that sidelined him for a considerable time and he was also embroiled in scandal and divorce. But who would dare bet against him rising again?

It has been the misfortune of the likes of Phil Mickelson, Ernie Els, Colin Montgomerie and Sergio Garcia to be part of the Tiger generation, for there is no saying how many majors they might have won but for the presence of the phenomena that is Woods, albeit Mickelson and Els have not done badly with nine between them.

Meanwhile, we must wait to discover if the precocious talent of Rory McIlroy makes him the natural successor to the player perceived by many to be the best golfer ever.

The Gear

Sporting gear was a bit more formal – and probably a lot more uncomfortable – in 1860.

THE computer age and advances in new technology means today's golfer is spoiled for choice when purchasing top-of-the-range-equipment.

Golf has also spawned a fashion industry to rival Savile Row, with the world's top players as equally suited to the cat walk as they are to the golf course.

But it wasn't always like that. One hundred and fifty years ago the necessities to play the game of ball and club were basic, to say the least.

Fashion wise, plus-fours and a stout pair of shoes were about as trendy as it got for the early pioneers of the game.

Go back much further to the Middle Ages and a pebble and a stick were all the very earliest players had to try and perfect their skills.

It's said that a group of sheep herders tending their flocks near St Andrews became proficient at knocking round stones into rabbit holes with their wooden crooks.

The first documented reference to a set of clubs was ones made for King James IV of Scotland in 1502, which were produced by his bow maker.

More than two centuries later the iron-headed "Putting Cleek" was produced along with several wooden-headed clubs with wood shafts by a club maker by the name of Simon Cossar from Leith.

But most players of the time built their own clubs from a variety of woods. The club heads were carved from hardwoods such as oak, cherry, beech and apple wood, while the shafts were made from softer, more flexible woods like ash or hazel wood.

It wasn't until the 19th Century that a Scot, Robert Forgan changed the way in which clubs were made. He used American hickory instead of the traditional ash or hazel wood to make his shafts and set the standard for club makers everywhere.

When Robert Simpson, from Earlsferry, Fife, produced a persimmon wood driver with a hickory shaft and a sheepskin grip in his workshop at Carnoustie the club was regarded as a major innovation and the persimmon-head spoon (3-wood) with a brass sole plate, hickory shaft and leather grip soon followed.

Various blacksmiths made iron head clubs and these were eventually produced in factories on a mass scale in the latter part of the 19th Century.

Andrew Kirkaldy, a three-time runner-up in the Open, is credited with the development of the Mashie (7-iron). Other iron headed clubs included the Rutting Iron, used to extract balls that landed in cart wheel tracks, the Cleek (1-iron), Mid Iron (5-iron), Mashie Niblick (9-iron), Niblick (Sand wedge) and putter.

Wooden headed clubs had tended to be made by individual club makers until around 1910. These included the Playclub (driver),

Victorian ladies pose for the camera before a round on the Old Course – note the stylish hats, white blouses and long skirts. The first Ladies Club was formed at St Andrews in 1867.

Steel shafts had been introduced in 1925 and had the advantage that they did not break like the hickory shafts and could be produced reliably with uniform feel in matched sets.

But the game's ruling body, the Royal & Ancient Golf Club of St Andrews was at first reluctant to sanction the use of steel shafts and it was only after the Prince of Wales used them on the Old Course in 1929 that they were given the seal of approval.

Immediately prior to the outbreak of the Second World War the R&A also decreed the use of no more than 14 clubs for a round, a ruling that has remained in place since.

The completion of the Second World War saw the development of golf clubs become heavily influenced by research carried out on composite and synthetic materials.

The first cast-made clubs appeared in the early sixties offering golfers an opportunity to purchase inexpensive clubs manufactured to high specifications and standards while the professionals continued to use the more traditional forged clubs as it was thought they offered an increased feel and control over cast clubs.

In 1972 graphite shafted clubs were introduced to the market offering exceptional rigidity, lightness and incomparable strength compared to steel shafted clubs. This type of shaft is commonly mixed with other materials to further improve performance.

The arrival on the scene of so-called metal woods was hailed as the biggest breakthrough in golf club manufacture to date. The first manufacturer of these clubs was Taylor-Made, but Callaway produced the most successful brand, the oversized Big Bertha, introduced in 1991.

The club heads were die cast with a hollow centre and filled with high density foam material, which increased the weight of the club head, making it similar in weight to smaller wooden club heads.

The greatest attraction of the metal woods

Scraper (3-wood), Long Spoon (3-wood), Middle Spoon (4-wood), Short Spoon (5-wood), Baffing Spoon (7-wood) and Niblick (9-wood). Eventually factories also started producing sets in large numbers.

By 1900, persimmon had replaced beech and other hard woods as the material of choice for club heads. But a popular alternative was aluminium in keeping with the tradition of hard forging club heads and in 1902 groove-faced irons appeared for the first time in one of the most important changes in design as they give increased backspin and greater distance.

In 1931 Billy Burke became the first golfer to win the US Open using steel-shafted clubs painted to look like wood while Gene Sarazen developed the sand wedge the following year and used it to win the Open.

▶

with adjustable over-sized driver heads is the increase in the area of the "sweet spot" allowing for a greater margin of forgiveness, increased distance and consistency.

However, the R&A and the United States Golf Association placed limitations on the size of clubheads, in particular due to the technological advances of drivers in an effort to curb distances and protect course lengths.

Fairway Hybrid irons and woods, also commonly referred to as "rescue clubs" that combine aspects of irons and woods, have also increased in popularity since their introduction a little over a decade ago.

They are distance clubs with a relatively long shaft that helps generate distance. Unlike the driver, a fairway metal has a sizeable degree of loft and this helps generate more height and backspin, which in turn counteracts sidespin, making it easier to hit straight.

Fairway woods and metals are regularly used for placement shots off the tee on par-4 holes and for advancement shots on long par-5s.

Irons have come a long way since the days of the Mashie Niblick, both in terms of design and accuracy. Blade-style clubheads have been largely superseded by more sophisticated cavity-back heads, stronger, easier to hit, better balanced, more consistent, and more forgiving.

They range from a 3-iron to a 9-iron and pitching wedge and have various degrees of loft. A player's swing and physical strength determine distance, but a long-iron (3-iron up to a 5) has a lower trajectory and carry approximately 80-yards more than a pitching wedge.

The shorter irons and wedges are used for approach shots to the green, chipping and bunker shots and call for precision play.

Most golfers are familiar with the expression, "Drive for show, putt for dough" and American engineer, Karsten Solheim created a putter in his garage in 1959 that made the latter just a little easier.

Solheim's creation had more weight at the heel and toe of the blade and a thinner, lighter sweet spot, making it easier to hit the ball straight. He subsequently quit his job and established the "Ping" brand. He came up with the name after testing the putter out and it produced a loud "pinging" sound.

It is a measure of the impact Ping putters have had on the game that more than 2,000 professional wins have been achieved using one.

The market in putters is huge and they range from conventional, to broomhandle, to belly and come in all shapes and designs of putting head. But golf's governing bodies have decreed that from January 2016 anchoring a club against any part of the body will be outlawed.

In a world of Fiberglas, Titanium, Graphite and Zirconia the rules still apply and must be strictly adhered to.

In January 2010, the R&A and the USGA implemented a new ruling on the size of club face groves in an effort to limit distance, initially enforcing the ruling only at major championships and tour events.

For the recreational player, irons made before 2010 will conform to the Rules of Golf until at least 2024.

Research had indicated that sharper, deeper groves in irons produced so much spin that players could hit the rough and still control iron shots to the green.

The size of the groves had to be made slightly smaller and have rounded edges instead of sharp edges on wedges through 5-irons to reduce spin.

Jim Furyk, one of the leading American players, welcomed the ruling, pointing out: "They can't keep making golf courses longer, because not every club has the budget to do so and they can't keep us from hitting the ball far, because there's enough engineers and technology that keeps us getting longer. So if you can limit the amount of spin on the ball and make the guy play from the fairway, it's probably a good move."

Fellow Ryder Cup player Phil Mickelson agreed, adding: "I feel like it's a challenging thing for a player to judge shots out of the first cut of rough or out of the rough. Is the ball going to spin? How is it going to come out?"

The evolution of the golf ball spreads over 500 years and the first known balls were made of wood, probably Beech or Boxroot in the 1400s.

It wasn't until the early 1700s that balls known as "Featheries" were introduced. They consisted of a leather outer shell stuffed with goose or chicken feathers. Several pieces of leather were stitched together, leaving a small opening for the feathers, which had been boiled and softened to make them more pliable, to be inserted in the casing before the final stitches were applied. The ball was then hammered into a round shape and finally coated with several layers of paint.

Due to the difficulty of producing these balls and the time involved in making Featheries, they were relatively expensive. But this type of ball was used for several hundred years before the first gutta-percha ball was developed midway through the 19th Century.

The "Gutta" or "Gutty" ball is believed to have been developed by the Rev. Dr. Robert Adams Paterson in 1848 and was a huge improvement on its predecessor, the Feathery.

Gutta-percha is the evaporated milk juice or latex produced from the tree of the same name found mainly in Malaysia. It is hard and non-brittle and becomes soft and impressible at the temperature of boiling water. The balls were handmade by rolling the softened material on a board.

The design was later improved by hammering the gutta to give the ball a more even pattern that improved its flight and run. This type of ball could reach a maximum distance of 225 yards and was similar to its modern counterpart in appearance.

The best-known balls were those produced by the Scottish club makers such as Allan Robertson, Old Tom Morris and the Auchterlonie family of St Andrews and the bramble pattern with a surface similar to the berry became the most popular of the era and was also used on some of the early rubber balls.

Perhaps the invention of the rubber ball was the single biggest change in golf. It was invented in 1898 by a Cleveland, Ohio golfer, Coburn Haskell and featured rubber thread wound around a solid rubber core. The creation of the Balata cover, developed in the early 1900s, was another significant step forward. It was said that the first rubber balls could reach distances of up to 430 yards.

The aerodynamically superior dimple pattern was first used in 1905 by manufacturer William Taylor, but it wasn't until 1930 that the British Golf Association set a standard of golf ball weight and size. Two years later the United States Golf Association set a standard for a slightly bigger, heavier ball.

In fact, between 1931 and 1988 the R&A sanctioned ball was 1.62in, slightly smaller than the now universal American/USGA ball of 1.68in. It meant that the leading professionals from the PGA Tour and the European Tour had to play with an unfamiliar golf ball when competing overseas.

The dimensions and weight of the modern ball is still strictly monitored by the game's governing ▶

bodies and a ball must not weigh more than 1.62oz and must have a diameter of at least 1.68in (4.6cm).

Some balls have softer cover made out of urethane for improved feel while others are manufactured from surlyn for a slightly harder texture. The core of the ball varies and is a mixture of synthetic rubbers and special compounds. Balls are one piece, two piece, three piece, or even four piece.

The R&A and the USGA also limit the maximum initial velocity to prevent balls travelling too far to preserve the integrity of golf courses.

Although there are no rules governing the number of dimples on a ball, most manufacturers use between 300 and 500 so patterns vary to a degree and influence the trajectory of the ball's flight, how high or low it flies and how much it spins and swerves.

A golf ball can be broken down into roughly three categories, distance, compromise and control although many of the manufacturers offer a hybrid mix.

The durability and precision of today's ball reflects not only the tremendous technological advancement in their manufacture but also the development of space age plastics, silicone and improved rubber.

But earthlings can only dream of emulating astronaut Alan Shepard's feat in 1971 when he hit two golf balls on the moon at the end of the Apollo 14 mission – one of them over a mile!

The modern caddie may appear at times as if he is carrying the weight of the world on his shoulders in the shape of the bulky tour bags used by the professionals displaying various sponsors' names by way of adding to the massive financial inducements that come from advertising. But the modern caddie has it easy compared to the original "bagmen".

It wasn't until the 1880s that caddies had bags to shoulder after previously having been forced to carry a player's clubs bound up with twine or string.

Powered carts are a common sight at most golf clubs but it wasn't until 1962 that they first appeared, having been invented by one Merlin L. Halvorson.

The word "tee" relates to the area where a golfer plays his first shot at each hole and golf tees appear in all shapes, sizes and materials and most nowadays are also personalised.

But 150 years ago it was usual for the caddie to make a small mound from earth or sand on which to place the ball. It wasn't until 1889 that the first documented portable golf tee was patented by Scottish golfers William Bloxsom and Arthur Douglas.

Made with rubber with three vertical prongs that held the ball in place, it lay on the ground and did not pierce the surface like modern golf tees.

But in 1892 a British patent was granted to Percy Ellis for a tee that did pierce the ground. It was made of rubber with a metal spike. Five years later Scotsman PM Matthews invented the first tee with a cup-shaped top to hold the ball more securely.

The rest, as they say, is history! ■

The Duel in the Sun

Jack Nicklaus (R) of the USA and Tom Watson (USA) joint leaders with a score of 203 after the 3rd round in the British Open golf championship at Turnberry in 1977.

THE history of golf is full of tales of intriguing head-to-head encounters, but none surpasses what has come to be known as the "Duel in the Sun."

No one could have foreseen the drama that unfolded on a glorious Saturday afternoon in the summer of 1977, when Turnberry hosted its first Open Championship.

The greatest golfers on the planet rolled up in South Ayrshire to contest the 106th championship between July 6 and 9th unfamiliar with their surroundings and the Ailsa Course which offers some of the most breathtaking views in golf across the Firth of Clyde.

By the time they departed the name "Turnberry" was forever etched on their minds after they had witnessed what is generally regarded as the most fascinating and brilliant head-to-head of all time.

The prize-fund was a tiny fraction of what it is today, totalling £100,000, with £10,000 of that earmarked as the winner's share.

But that did not deter the Americans from jetting across the Atlantic in pursuit of the oldest major in golf, among them the finest player of his generation and a worthy rival for the crown.

Three months earlier, Tom Watson had held off Jack Nicklaus at Augusta to win his first Masters, but there were still some who doubted the younger man.

In the end the Americans dominated the leaderboard, filling the top 11 spots. But two stood head and shoulders above the rest in a field of 12 past champions.

John Schroeder of the United States led after round one, by a shot from England's Martin Foster with Nicklaus and Watson equal third with compatriot Lee Trevino, one shot further back after opening with 68s.

Another American, Roger Maltbie replaced Schroeder as leader the following day, with four players, Hubert Green, Nicklaus, Trevino and Watson grouped together one off the pace. But the most notable achievement was that of their countryman, Mark Hayes who carded a 63 to establish a new single round record in the Open by two strokes.

A total of 69 players fell by the wayside at halfway, leaving 87 survivors from the first cut. When play ended on day three that number was further reduced to 64 and the stage was set for a dramatic finish with Nicklaus and Watson tied for the lead at seven-under-par following matching 65s.

While the championship had not quite developed into a two-horse race, the leading duo had established a sizeable advantage of three shots over their closest rival, countryman Ben Crenshaw. The rest were largely nowhere, six shots adrift.

So Nicklaus, already a two-time Open champion, and Watson, winner at Carnoustie two years earlier, were poised to fight a duel to the death.

Nicklaus, 37, was the game's acknowledged master, a winner of 14 major championships. Watson, a decade younger, was the reigning Masters champion. It was also the methodical Nicklaus versus the fast-swinging, scrambling Watson.

And by the fourth hole it appeared that the eagerly anticipated duel was fast developing into a tame surrender as Nicklaus – the bookmakers' ▶

favourite and the crowd's also – built a three-shot lead.

Both men having parred the first, Nicklaus birdied the second while Watson made bogey for a two-shot swing. Another birdie at the fourth to Watson's par had the Golden Bear circling his prey menacingly.

But Watson was not the type to run up the white flag of surrender and the tide quickly turned. Watson birdied the fifth and the seventh while his opponent could only manage pars and by the eighth it was all-square.

Watson's birdie putt at the eighth put a dent in the cup and he was later gracious enough to admit: "I was lucky. If it wasn't dead centre, it would have gone six or seven feet by the hole."

As the two golfing musketeers headed for the picturesque lighthouse, Nicklaus regained the lead when Watson dropped a shot at the ninth to turn one in front.

The following gallery, thousands strong, had broken through the ropes on the ninth fairway and sprinted past the players in what was little more than a stampede. It took stewards quarter-of-an-hour to clear the fairway, during which time Nicklaus sat on his bag and Watson stood nearby.

"I remember Jack kindly asking the stewards to get the crowds under control, but there was something of a frenzy" Watson recalled. "We didn't converse, we just waited. There's nothing you can do in that situation."

The interruption to play appeared to have a greater effect on Watson, given that he bogeyed the hole and turned in 34. But the next two holes were halved at the start of the back nine.

Then Nicklaus sank a 22-footer for birdie at 12 to lead again by two. But the duel continued to rage and with each thrust and parry the tension and excitement grew almost to fever pitch.

Watson responded with a 12-foot birdie on 13 and it was obvious that he just would not go way, regardless of Nicklaus' icy stare and mighty reputation.

Standing on the 14th tee waiting for the crowds to once again be brought under control, Watson turned to Nicklaus and said: "This is what it's all about, isn't it?" and his rival replied: "You bet it is."

Watson later added: "We were looking into the sun in the western sky, the crowd created a cloud of dust and it reminded me of 'Golf in the Kingdom,' of spirituality in the game of golf. It was one of those moments."

The 14th was halved in pars, but not even Watson could have anticipated what happened next. His 60-foot putt from off the 15th green hopped in the air, raced across the putting surface, smacked the flagstick and dropped into the hole for a birdie two.

It was an arrow through Nicklaus' heart. "It was

Turnberry – the venue for the famous "Duel in the Sun" in 1977.

one of many putts in my career that broke other players' hearts," said Watson. "It changed the momentum of the round for Jack and it changed the momentum of the round for me.

"A lot goes into making a long putt and I was pretty good at it. It's a God-given thing. You can't teach 'feel' for the game."

With what had long become a match-play duel once again all-square the crowd erupted as the players made their way to the 16th tee.

With two holes to play the outcome was balanced on a knife edge after the 16th had been shared in par-4s.

But it was Watson who struck at the penultimate hole to set up victory. A drive, a 3-iron and two putts earned him a birdie at the par-5 while Nicklaus stunned himself and the watching world by missing a three-footer and having to settle for par.

At the last Watson's 1-iron off the tee found an ideal position on the fairway, but Nicklaus went right into the rough. Watson then sent his 7-iron approach two-feet left of the flag and, with Nicklaus in trouble, appeared to be on the cusp of victory.

"Before I played I went over to see Jack's ball, to see if he had a shot, to see if it was playable," Watson remembered. "He was six inches from unplayable, but he had a swing and only one person in the world could play that shot and it was Jack Nicklaus.

The Champ – Tom Watson's victory stroll across the 18th green.

"I went back to my ball. I had 178 yards. I had a 7-iron and I hit it right on the nose, just left of the hole. I knew it was close. I didn't know how close. Then I watched Jack play his shot.

"He took at least a square yard of sod. It was a mighty swing and the ball came out tumbling as it always does from heavy grass. It bounced short and I thought it would kick right but it kicked straight on to the green and the crowd came together like the Red Sea.

"My caddie, Alfie Fyles said: 'You've got it now, mister' but I replied: 'Jack's going to make that putt' and Alfie looked at me almost cross-eyed. He couldn't believe it. But I learned playing golf all of my life not to ever assume someone won't make the best shot possible."

Nicklaus was not quite done. Having slashed his 8-iron recovery onto the front of the green, he sank his 35-foot putt for a remarkable birdie and a blemish-free 66.

The crowd was in a fresh frenzy and they continued to cheer until Nicklaus raised his hands and the deafening roars fell silent.

Watson now needed to sink his two-footer to avoid an 18-hole play-off and duly did for his second straight 65, second Open and third major title. His total of 268 was also eight strokes better than the previous best score ever in an Open.

It was a measure of how far removed they were from their rivals after shooting the same score every day except for Saturday that the third place finisher, reigning US Open champion Hubert Green was a distant 10 strokes behind Nicklaus.

Green, who had once described Watson as a "very marginal player and a great collapser" must have risked choking on humble pie!

In a memorable act of true sportsmanship Nicklaus threw his arms around the champion's shoulders and walked him towards the scorer's tent.

Turnberry and 30,000 Scots had witnessed history in the making. Millions more TV viewers had sat transfixed.

Surely South Ayrshire would never again play host to such compelling drama. But history, in a sense, very nearly repeated itself 32 years later.

There was only one swordsman in July 2009, but Tom Watson relived that glorious summer day at the age of 59 – only for fate to cruelly decree at the very last moment that one of the greatest sports stories of all time would not be written with a perfect ending. ■

The Great Ladies of Golf

THE growth in women's golf over the past four decades has been nothing short of phenomenal.

A regular feature of television coverage of the sport, the top women players have become as easily identifiable as their male counterparts.

According to a recent survey, women are the fastest growing segment of new players, with more than six million female golfers in the United States alone. But it took the women's game almost 400 years to become firmly established on the world stage.

Yet, women's golf had the seal of Royal approval as far back as the 1550s, when Mary, Queen of Scots, is credited with commissioning the building of the first golf course at St Andrews to satisfy her need to play the game. She reportedly also coined the term "caddies" by calling her assistants "cadets."

But it wasn't until the 1860s that the first ladies golf club was formed. The women players of St Andrews founded The Ladies Club and more soon followed at Musselburgh, Wimbledon and Carnoustie.

In 1891 The Shinnecock Hills Golf Club on Long Island opened its doors to women members and followed up by creating a nine-hole course for the exclusive use of the fairer sex two years later.

The development of women's competitive golf in Britain was assisted greatly by the formation of the Ladies Golf Union and its inaugural championship in 1893.

The following year the first ladies tournament in the USA was staged on the seven-hole Morristown, New Jersey course and the United States Golf Association was formed, initially as The Amateur Golf Association of the United States.

Twelve months later the first US Women's Amateur Championship was held at the Meadow Brook Club in Hempstead, New York.

In Britain, meanwhile, the growth in the women's game was gathering speed at a slightly more genteel pace, but the arrival on the scene of Cecil Leitch and Joyce Wethered in the early years of the 20th Century did much to focus greater attention on female golfers.

Born at Silloth, Cumbria, Leitch and Wethered, from Surrey, advanced both the standard and the popularity of the women's game, most notably through their great rivalry, which became front-page news.

In 1908, at the age of just 17, Leitch caused quite a stir when she reached the semi-finals of the British Ladies Amateur Championship. Two years later she won a 72-hole challenge against Harold Hilton, the two-time Open champion, after receiving a stroke a hole.

A long and straight hitter, Leitch confirmed her status as the top woman player by winning the first of five French titles in 1912. She was also British

Cecil Leitch competing at the Ladies Golf Cup in 1914.

© Hulton-Deutsch Collection/Corbis

Ladies Amateur champion four times, in addition to taking the Canadian title in 1921.

The younger Wethered equalled Leitch's tally in the British Ladies Amateur Championship, also winning five English Ladies Championships to succeed her great rival as the best woman player of the time.

It was a measure of Wethered's talents that when she played a match against the great Bobby Jones at St Andrews in 1930, she scored 75 playing off the back tees in a breeze.

Afterwards Jones was moved to declare: "I have not played golf with anyone, man or woman, amateur or professional, who made me feel so utterly outclassed. It was not so much the score she made as the way she made it. It was impossible to expect that Miss Wethered would ever miss a shot – and she never did."

The brother of Roger, an Amateur champion and the runner-up in the 1921 Open, Joyce Wethered was said to possess perfect equilibrium.

Around the same time as Leitch and Wethered were in their pomp, Glenna Collett Vare, from Connecticut, dominated the woman's game in America, winning the US Amateur title six times, the Canadian twice and the French in 1925.

Following the foundation of The Professional Golfers' Association of America in 1916, the Women's Tournament Committee of the USGA was

Joyce Wethered – said to possess perfect equilibrium.

In a remarkable career spanning three decades, the American won more than 80 titles as an amateur and professional, including a record 15 majors championships and the first US Women's Open.

Berg also introduced her own "signature" clubs and encouraged thousands to take up the game by giving clinics and exhibitions and was the driving force behind the formation of the Women's Professional Golf Association (WPGA) in 1944. It was replaced by the Ladies Professional Golf Association (LPGA) six years later.

In a golden age of talent, Babe Zaharias – formerly Mildred Didrikson, one of seven children of Norwegian immigrants – was arguably the most colourful and accomplished woman athelete of all time.

Prior to focussing her talents on golf, Zaharias played a variety of sports to an exceptionally high standard, notably baseball, hitting so many home runs that she earned the nickname "Babe" after Babe Ruth and the name stuck.

At trials for the 1932 Olympics she entered eight events, won six and set four world records. At the subsequent Los Angeles Games she won gold in the javelin and 80m hurdles and silver in the high jump.

The multi-talented Texan then turned to golf, winning her first amateur event in 1935. She went on to revolutionise the women's game and was such a powerful hitter that none of her rivals could match her for distance.

To give some indication of Zaharias' power, when she played against the men in the 1945 L.A. Open she made two of the first three cuts.

Married to a wrestler of Greek descent, Zaharias once compiled an astonishing run of 27 victories from 28 events and was both the US Women's Amateur champion and the British Ladies Amateur champion – the first American to achieve the feat – as well US Women's Open champion on three occasions.

The star of the new LPGA circuit, Zaharias averaged one win in every four of the events she played before her untimely death at the age of just 45 in 1956.

The third star of the women's game when the LPGA was born in 1950 was Louise Suggs, from Atlanta. The daughter of a former pitcher for the New York Yankees, she was credited with having a smooth and rhythmic swing of beauty.

Winner of the US Women's Amateur and the British Ladies Amateur, Suggs won 55 times as a pro, including 11 majors, and was a founder member of the LPGA.

The first nationally televised event – the 1963 US Women's Open – coincided with Californian Mickey Wright at the peak of her remarkable powers.

A perfectionist who had a swing that was the envy of her rivals and greatly admired by her male ▶

formed a year later and by 1932 the strength of the game on both sides of the pond was such that it was decided to stage a biennial match between the women amateur golfers of the USA and those of Great Britain and Ireland. Known as the Curtis Cup, the USA were the first winners.

When Helen Hicks became one of the first women golfers to turn professional in 1934 there were no professional tournaments and she financed herself by promoting sports goods.

What more Jessie Valentine might have achieved but for the intervention of the Second World War is impossible to say, but "Wee Jessie", as she was known, still dominated women's amateur golf for two decades either side of the conflict.

From Perth, Valentine won the British Ladies Amateur Championship three times, including a gap of 18 years between 1937 and 1955, and was Scottish champion on six occasions. She was also the first woman to be honoured for her services to golf when she was awarded an MBE, later also becoming a member of the Scottish Sport Hall of Fame prior to her death at the age of 91 in 2006.

Patty Berg's career ran parallel to that of Valentine's. A pioneer of women's professional golf, Berg won the first Titleholders Championships for professional and amateur female golfers in 1937 and repeated the feat six more times.

counterparts, Wright – tall and attractive with a winning smile – was perhaps the first true superstar of women's golf.

In 1961 she won three of her 13 majors in a season and two years later won a record 13 times, finally amassing a total of 82 LPGA victories, the last of them in 1973.

The year before the LPGA celebrated the landmark of the first six-figure purse in women's golf, when $110,000 was on offer at the Colgate-Dinah Shore Championship. Four years later, in 1976, Judy Rankin became the first LPGA player to earn in excess of $100,000 in a season when she pocketed $150,734 in prize-money.

In another significant step in the development of the ladies' game, in 1977 The PGA of America voted to accept female members.

The LPGA had been in existence for 29 years by the time Europe caught up and formed a similar organisation in an effort to develop the women's game and increase opportunities for professionals.

In 1978 the Women's Professional Golf Association (WPGA) was formed as part of the Professional Golfers' Association of Great Britain and Ireland and a tour was established the following year.

Getting a women's tour established in Europe was not easy. Whereas men's golf had developed in parallel with the United States, the women's tour had to compete against a well established rival in the LPGA from its foundation.

In 1988 the tour members decided to form an independent company, the Women Professional Golfers' European Tour Limited, moving from the PGA's headquarters at The Belfry and setting up its own offices in Cheshire.

There were two further changes of name, in 1998, when the WPGET became the European Ladies Professional Golf Association Limited, and again in July 2000 to its current title, Ladies European Tour Limited or LET for short.

The new-look tour developed gradually and by 2008 had a record 28 official ranking tournaments. That figure has fluctuated slightly due to the recent economic climate, but has remained relatively stable since 2010.

The two richest events are the Evian Championship and the Women's British Open, which are co-sanctioned by the LPGA Tour and have prize funds of about £3.8million. The total prize-fund is in the region of £9million.

Unlike the men's game, the European and American tours don't share a common set of majors. But the Women's British Open has been recognised as a major by both organisations, and the Evian Championship, held in France and a LET major since its inception in 1994, became an LPGA major as well in 2013.

In addition to the British Open and the Evian,

Laura Davies putts on the first hole during the final round of the Safeway Classic at Pumpkin Ridge Golf Club August 22, 2010 in North Plains, Oregon.

the US Open, the LPGA Championship and the Kraft Nabisco Championship make up the five women's majors, one more than their male counterparts.

The emergence of a pretty and bubbly teenager from California in the mid-1970s helped raise the LPGA's profile. In her first full season Nancy Lopez won five tournaments in a row and nine in all. She also became the first female golfer to earn both the Rookie of the Year and LPGA Player of the Year honours in the same season.

But in 1981 it was Kathy Whitworth who became the first woman golfer to top $1million in career earnings, also surpassing Mickey Wright's record of 82 LPGA wins and eventually going on to establish an all-time record of official victories for women and men of 88.

A decade later Juli Inkster, another Californian, struck a blow for the women when she upstaged the men by winning the only professional golf tournament in the world in which both sexes competed head-to-head in an Invitational Pro-Am.

The Solheim Cup was also born in 1990, pitting the professional women players of Europe and America against each other. The Americans swept to victory in the inaugural match, by 11½ points to 4½, but they did not have it all their own way on the world scene.

A tall, powerfully built English woman challenged the might of her

© Troy Wayrynen/NewSport/Corbis

largely to an indifferent putting performance.

Sorenstam was also the leading Solheim Cup points scorer until overtaken by Davies in 2011 and the first player to shoot 59 on the LPGA Tour.

Her crown as world number one was eventually transferred to a delightful Mexican, but Lorena Ochoa's reign was comparatively short-lived. At the peak of her powers, she announced that she was retiring from the sport at the age of just 28 to focus on her family.

By then Ochoa had captured the hearts of golf fans everywhere with her warm, friendly personality, and, in addition to the Women's British Open title in 2007, she won a second major, the Kraft Nabisko Championship the following year.

And in the three years she dominated the women's game she rarely finished tournaments outside the top-10, winning 27 in total.

Ochoa's victory at St Andrews in 2007 held special significance as it was the first time the home of golf had hosted a prestigious woman's event and the R&A had thrown open its doors to the fairer sex. The Women's British Open subsequently returned to the Old Course in 2013.

Judy Bell's appointment as the first woman president of the United States Golf Association in 1996 also broke new ground, as did the LPGA's success in brokering a deal two years later for the first ever sponsored television series in women's golf, including seven LPGA tournaments offering a bonus pool of $250,000 to players.

While Tiger Woods can be said to have dominated the men's game in a way that no other has done, with the possible exception of Jack Nicklaus, no one woman player has enjoyed similar longevity as the leader of the pack.

But Karie Webb was once described by fellow Australian and five-time Open champion Peter Thomson as the best golfer on the planet – man or woman, with a swing better than that of Tiger Woods – during her prime years between 1999 and 2003, when she won six majors, including five out of eight.

Se Ri Pak, leader of the Korean invasion, was another who took the women's game by storm ahead of her compatriots who have applied a powerful stranglehold: players like Inbee Park, Birdie Kim, Eun –Hee Ji, So Yeon Ryu, Grace Park, Jeong Jang, Jiyai Shin, Na Yeon Choi, Shanshan Feng of China and Taiwan's Yani Tseng.

Norway's Suzann Pettersen, America's Stacey Lewis and Lexi Thompson and Lydia Ko of New Zealand are others from the current generation who continue to face stiff competition from the likes of Paula Creamer, Cristie Kerr and Morgan Pressel, from the United States.

At the age of just 10 in 2000, a golfing phenomenon burst onto the scene. Michelle Wie,

rivals worldwide and came out on top. Laura Davies, born in Coventry in October 1963, followed up her victory in the 1986 Women's British Open by capturing the American equivalent 12 months later and was also LPGA champion in 1994 and '96, the same year she won the Du Murier Classic.

Davies, a stalwart of the Solheim Cup, also led Europe to a stunning victory in the first match to be played on Scottish soil, at Dalmahoy, Edinburgh in 1992, 11½-6½, and was a key member of the winning teams at Loch Lomond, Sweden and Ireland in subsequent matches with an unbroken run of 12 appearances up to and including 2011.

A seven-time winner of the Ladies European Tour order of merit title, Davies has been a prolific winner across four decades, capturing in excess of 80 titles, including victories in Europe, America, India, Australia, New Zealand, Japan and Asia and was recognised as the best female player in the world in the mid-1990s.

But then along came an ice-cool Swede by the name of Annika Sorenstam to take the ladies game to new levels of excellence. Born near Stockholm in 1970, Sorenstam retired at the age of 38 having won 93 times worldwide, including 10 majors, earning $22 million in the process.

Recognised as one of the finest woman players of all time, she also became the first since Babe Zaharias to compete in an event on the men's tour, in 2003 at Colonial, where she missed the cut by four strokes due the Hawaiian-born child of South Korean immigrant parents, became the youngest player to qualify for a USGA amateur championship. She also became the youngest winner of the US Women's Amateur Public Links Championship and the youngest to qualify for an LPGA Tour event.

Having begun playing the game at the age of just four, Wie's talents blossomed to the extent that in 2001, when still only 11-years-old, she won both the Hawaii State Women's Stroke Play Championship and the Jennie K. Wilson Women's Invitational, the oldest and most prestigious women's amateur tournament in Hawaii. Two years later she won the US Women's Amateur Public Links Championship at Palm Coast, Florida.

Golf had never seen anyone like her and when she qualified for the LPGA's Takefuji Classic in her home state in 2002 she was hailed as potentially the most exciting talent in the history of the game.

Although she missed the cut, the following year Wie qualified to play in the final group in the Kraft Nabisco Championship, also making the cut in the US Women's Open.

That same year, Suzy Walley, an LPGA and PGA professional, became the first woman to qualify for a PGA Tour event, the Greater Hartford Open.

Having been given a sponsor's exemption to the 2004 Sony Open in Hawaii, Wie became the youngest female to compete in a PGA Tour event and her second round 68 was the lowest score ever recorded by a woman. That same year she finished fourth in the Kraft Nabisco Championship and also became the youngest woman ever to play in the Curtis Cup, helping the United States to victory.

In 2005 Wie again played in the Sony Open and another PGA Tour event, the John Deere Classic, missing the cut in both, in addition to five LPGA events.

It was only a question of time before Wie turned professional and she did so in October 2005, a week before her 16th birthday. She also signed sponsorship contracts with Nike and Sony reportedly worth more than $10million a year.

But it wasn't going to be a case of instant success for the 6ft 1in teenager who was unable to secure LPGA membership as she was under the minimum age of 18. By the end of her first full year in the paid ranks she had missed the cut in 11 of the 12 starts against men and was winless in 33 women's professional tournaments.

The increasing level of expectancy became a growing burden for Wie and she attracted widespread criticism when she retired from the LPGA's Ginn Tribute, citing an aggravated wrist injury when 14-over par after 16 holes. Under LPGA rules, a non-member shooting a score of 88 or more is forced to withdraw and is subsequently banned from LPGA co-sponsored events for the rest of the year.

Michelle Wie in action during the second round of the Evian Masters Golf Tournament, on July 27, 2012.

A year-long streak of 24 consecutive rounds of par or worse ended at the Evian Masters in July 2007, when she shot a second round one-under-par 71. But a week later, at the British Open at St Andrews, she crashed out at halfway, her first missed cut in an LPGA event since 2003, and her first missed cut in a major.

At the same time compatriot Morgan Pressel, just 18, became the youngest woman to win an LPGA major tournament at the Kraft Nabisco Championship.

Wie's failure to achieve a maiden victory as a pro was offset by the revelation that her annual earnings were estimated to be $19million.

After qualifying to play full-time on the LPGA Tour in 2009, Wie continued to struggle, but at last, on November 15, she achieved the big breakthrough, winning the Lorena Ochoa Invitational in Guadalajara, Mexico.

The following August she claimed a three-shot victory in the CN Canadian Women's Open for her second career professional win. Tied second in the 2005 LPGA Championship remains her best result in a major to date.

But still only 24, Wie may still fulfil Arnold Palmer's prediction made in 2003 when the American legend declared: "She is probably going to influence the golfing scene as much as Tiger, or more."

© Manuel Blondeau/Corbis

in popularity, also given the regular television coverage it receives.

But perhaps two of the most significant developments have been Augusta's decision to admit female members and the R&A's willingness to examine in depth the issue of all-male clubs.

In August 2012 Augusta National invited women to play the course for the first time in its 80-year history after admitting former US Secretary of State Condoleezza Rice and South Carolina businesswoman Darla Moore as members.

The club had been the subject of protests by women's groups, but the issue really came to light when Augusta technically had to offer membership to Virginia Rometty, the first female CEO of IBM, as the club always offered admittance to that company's CEOs.

Tim Finchem, the PGA Tour commissioner, welcomed the groundbreaking move, adding: "At a time when women represent one of the fastest growing segments in both playing and following the game of golf, this sends a positive and inclusive message for our sport."

While Peter Dawson, chief executive of the R&A, expressed the view that single-sex clubs are a matter for each individual club, he also conceded: "We will have to look at what people are saying and try to take a view about all of this and find the most sensible way forward as we understand it's a polarizing issue."

Golf's governing body has come under increasing pressure from international business corporations such as HSBC, a major sponsor of the Open Championship and the European Tour, to address the issue, with the result that the R&A is now urging its 2,400 members to abolish their 260-year-old male-only policy.

An historic poll is to be held when a two-thirds majority is expected to vote in favour of admitting women members.

When making the announcement, Dawson said: "We very much hope the decision is taken to welcome women as members. Early indications are very positive indeed and it's appropriate for the governing body to take this step."

Three of the nine Open Championship venues – Muirfield, Royal St George's and Royal Troon – do not allow women members, but Dawson added: "We are not intending to place other golf clubs under any particular pressure by doing this.

"We have to put the needs of the Open high up our list of priorities and to lose a number of key venues would not seem to me to be doing that."

But as the wind of change continues to blow through golf some of the last bastions of male dominance in sporting establishments are coming under increasing threat of being toppled by "girl power." ◾

Fellow American Alexis "Lexi" Thompson has since set several new age records. At age 12, she was the youngest golfer ever to qualify to play in the US Women's Open before turning pro three years later.

And in September 2011, Thompson set a new record as the youngest-ever winner of an LPGA event, capturing the Navistar Classic, at age 16 years, seven months, and eight days. Just three months later she became the second youngest winner of a Ladies European Tour event, landing the Dubai Ladies Masters.

Still only 19, Thompson already has a total of five victories to her credit as well as finishing third in the Evian Championship in 2013.

Britain is also fortunate to have a special young talent in teenager Charley Hull, who turned professional in January 2013, making her debut on the Ladies European Tour two months later and reeling off five consecutive second place finishes.

The LET Rookie of the Year, from Kettering, Hull, born in March 1996, won her first professional title, the Lalla Meryem Cup in Morocco and represented Europe in the Solheim Cup victory over the United States as the youngest competitor in the history of the biennial match before her 18th birthday.

With talents such as Thompson and Hull gracing the current women's game it seems reasonable to assume that it will continue to grow

Gleneagles – the venue for the 2014 Ryder Cup.

IT is said that the Ryder Cup transcends sport, yet remains true to the spirit of its founder, Samuel Ryder.

In the television age the event attracts a global audience of tens of millions and cannot be matched for drama, tension, camaraderie and sportsmanship.

It started off as an informal match between Britain and America in 1921 at Gleneagles and has developed into a multi-million pound biennial clash which enthrals golf fans worldwide.

The origin of an international match between the best Great Britain professionals and those of America based on prestige rather than prize-money is unclear.

Sylvanus P. Jermain, president of Inverness Golf Club, Ohio is credited by some of presenting the concept. Others claim that it was the brainchild of a circulation representative of an American golf magazine, one James Harnett, who proposed the idea in an effort to increase circulation and was subsequently given financial backing by the U.S. PGA as well as the support of top American player Walter Hagen.

Regardless of who takes credit, the first informal match resulted in a 9-3 victory for the home team. A second unofficial match took place at Wentworth in 1926 and the Americans again lost, 13½-1½.

Samuel Ryder, a seed merchant and an entrepreneur from St Albans, was present at Wentworth. Born in 1858, Ryder, the son of a Manchester corn merchant, came to golf comparatively late in life after being advised by his doctor to take up the game to combat ill-health brought on by overwork and his civic duties as Mayor of St Albans.

Ryder employed the services of British star Abe Mitchell as his personal golf tutor at an annual fee of £1,000 and he boasted a six handicap at the age of 51. He later became captain of the Verulam Golf Club in St Albans, where he resided, and sponsored a tournament for professionals in 1923.

After Mitchell had beaten the reigning Open champion Jim Barnes,

Individual Ryder Cup Records

**MOST APPEARANCES
ON A TEAM: 11**
Nick Faldo (EUR/GB&I) 1977-97.

MOST POINTS WON: 25
Nick Faldo (EUR/GB&I).

**MOST SINGLE
POINTS WON: 7**
Colin Montgomerie (EUR)
Billy Casper (USA)
Lee Trevino (USA)
Arnold Palmer (USA)
Neil Coles (GB&I)

**MOST FOURSOME
POINTS WON: 11½**
Bernhard Langer (EUR)

**MOST FOURBALL
POINTS WON: 10½**
Ian Woosnam (EUR)
Jose Maria Olazabal (EUR)

YOUNGEST PLAYER:
Sergio Garcia (EUR)
19 years, 258 days in 1999

OLDEST PLAYER:
Raymond Floyd (USA)
51 years, 20 days 1993

8&7, at Wentworth and then partnered Scotsman George Duncan to a 9&8 victory against Hagen and Barnes in the foursomes, Ryder sought out the players.

He hosted a party for them at a nearby pub where they served champagne and chicken sandwiches. In addition he gave each member of the winning team £5.

During the evening, Duncan suggested Ryder provide a trophy and encourage the establishment of matches on a regular basis. Ryder duly agreed and commissioned the design of a gold cup in the shape of a chalice that bears his name and Mitchell's likeness on top.

The trophy was designed by London jewellers Mappin & Webb at a cost of £250 and the inaugural match was scheduled to take place in June, 1927, at the Worcester Country Club, Massachusetts.

An appeal for £3,000 to finance the British team had fallen £500 short of its goal and Ryder made up the deficit. The famed "Great Triumvirate" of Harry Vardon, J.H. Taylor and James Braid acted as the team selection committee.

The visiting team was robbed of its captain, Mitchell, who was suffering from appendicitis, and the hosts defeated their counterparts from Great Britain, 9½-2½ to gain revenge for their earlier losses in the unofficial matches.

The 2010 Ryder Cup – Celtic Manor Resort, Newport, Wales. The European Ryder Cup Team of Luke Donald, Lee Westwood, Martin Kaymer, Peter Hansen, Captain Colin Montgomerie, Padraig Harrington, Ross Fisher, Ian Poulter, Miguel Angel Jimenez, Francesco Molinari, Edoardo Molinari, Rory McILroy and Graeme McDowell celebrate with the Ryder Cup.

Two years later, at Moortown, Leeds the home side gained revenge, by dint of a 7-5 victory. Walter Hagen, the America captain, also suffered the embarrassment of a 10 and 8 defeat by his British counterpart George Duncan in the singles - a victory that helped turn the tables after the visitors had won the foursomes. It remains the biggest 36-hole singled margin in the history of the event.

Ryder lived to see two of the subsequent matches on his home soil before dying at the age of 77 in January, 1936 following a massive haemorrhage.

The early years of the Ryder Cup were fairly evenly contested with two wins apiece. But the 1933 match at Southport and Ainsdale very nearly did not take place.

Hagen, again the American captain, did not keep an appointed meeting with his opposite number, J.H. Taylor to exchange orders beforehand – or a second meeting. A third was arranged with Taylor issuing an ultimatum that, if Hagen defaulted again, he would call the match off and the world would know why. This time, Hagen kept his appointment and all was well.

From 1935 onwards the Americans began dominating the event to the extent that they won the next seven matches either side of the Second World War.

Unofficial matches were staged several times during the war years to raise funds, but it wasn't until 1947 after a gap of 10 years that the competition was resumed at Portland Golf Club, Oregon, where the home team scored a resounding 11-1 victory.

The Americans won the first 11 matches but Britain was spared the humiliation of a whitewash when Sam King won the final singles against Herman Keiser.

The Americans won the next four matches as well and it wasn't until 1957, at Lindrick Golf Club, Yorkshire, that Great Britain restored a modicum of pride with a 7½-4½ success. But it proved to be a one-off when the United States followed up by winning five-in-a-row.

From the beginning of the series through 1959, when the British party travelling from Los Angeles to Palm Beach had a narrow escape when their plane was hit by lightning during a thunderstorm, the Ryder Cup had comprised of four foursomes matches on one day and eight singles on the other, each of 36 holes.

That format was changed in 1961, to provide four 18-hole foursomes matches the morning of the first day, four more foursomes that afternoon, eight 18-hole singles the morning of the second day and eight

more singles that afternoon. One point was at stake in each match, so the total number of points was doubled to 24.

In 1963, fourball matches were added for the first time, boosting the total number of points available to 32, and the event expanded to three days.

There was a brief respite in Great Britain's suffering in 1969 at Royal Birkdale, Southport by way of a tied match, 16-16, after the team size had been increased from 10 to 12, but it was a familiar story in the subsequent seven matches.

When the Ryder Cup was contested for the first time in Scotland in 1973 at Muirfield the PGA altered its selection procedure by having eight players chosen from a year-long points system and four by invitation.

It was also decided to change the official title of the Great Britain team to "Great Britain and Ireland" to reflect the fact that golfers from Northern Ireland had competed since 1947 and others from the Republic of Ireland since 1953.

The playing format was altered again in 1977, this time with five foursomes on the opening day, five fourballs on the second day, and 10 singles matches on the final day, reducing the total points to 20.

But the new systems made little difference to the outcome when the USA won by five-and-a-half points and it became increasingly clear that further changes were necessary to restore a more competitive element to the biennial match.

This was done in 1979 when players from continental Europe were included for the first time, widening the competition's appeal and laying the foundation for the tide to start turning.

Jack Nicklaus had approached the PGA of Great Britain during the match at Royal Lytham & St Annes two years earlier to express concern that something radical had to be done to widen the selection procedures if the event was to be upgraded to retain its appeal and continue to enjoy its past prestige.

The playing format was also revised yet again in 1979 to provide four fourball and four foursomes matches on each of the first two days and 12 singles matches on the third day worth a total of 28 points, a format which continues to this day.

The first match under the new format was staged at The Greenbrier in Virginia and the first two Europeans to make the team were Seve Ballesteros and his compatriot Antonio Garrido.

▶

Ryder Cup American team winners 1977: Dow Finsterwald (front) with the trophy (USA Captain) L to R : Hubert Green, Ray Floyd, Dave Stockton, Lanny Wadkins, Tom Watson, Hale Irwin, Jerry McGee, Jack Nicklaus, Ed Sneed, Don January, Lou Graham, Dave Hill.

Ballesteros was to go on to become one of the most successful Ryder Cup players of all time, winning 20 times in eight appearances before also captaining Europe to victory in 1997.

But not even Ballesteros could deny the Americans again in 1979. They triumphed 17-11 and by nine points at Walton Heath two years later.

However, by 1983 the gap at the PGA National Golf Club, Florida had narrowed to a single point in favour of the hosts and hopes were high when the match returned to The Belfry two years later under Tony Jacklin's captaincy.

That optimism was fully justified when Europe claimed a 16½-11½ win followed by a successful defence at Muirfield Village 24 months later, their first ever success on American soil.

Following a tied match at The Belfry in 1989, when captain's picks or wildcards was used by both sides for the first time, America won the next two by narrow margins. But their 15-13 victory at The Belfry in 1993 also signalled the end of their years of almost total dominance.

The remarkable swing towards European dominance is highlighted by the fact that Europe has won no fewer than seven of the last nine matches, twice establishing record-equalling wins home and away, by 18½-9½ points, at Oakland Hill in 2004 and the K-Club, Ireland two years later, following the groundbreaking change in the selection process.

Europe has in fact been beaten only once since their controversial defeat at Brookline in 1999 when Sir Nick Faldo oversaw a 16½-11½ loss at Valhalla Golf club, Kentucky in 2008.

History was also made in 1997 when the match was staged on Continental Europe for the first time, at Valderrama Golf Club, Sotogrande, Spain where the late Ballesteros was the inspiration and driving force.

Two years later when the focus switched to The Country Club, Brookline, Massachusetts, the match was overshadowed by bad feeling, as it had been eight years earlier at Kiawah Island, South Carolina, and following "The War on the Shore" and "The Battle of Brookline" *(see page 85)* strenuous efforts were made to ensure that the sporting nature of the event was restored.

The Ryder Cup was interrupted for the second time in its history following the September 11, 2001 attack on America. Shortly after, the match at The Belfry was rescheduled for the following year, with all future competitions conducted in even-numbered years.

After an unprecedented run of just three wins in 11 matches since 1985, the fear was that the Americans were rapidly losing interest in the match. But their victory in 2008 changed that growing mindset.

United States captain Paul Azinger pulled a masterstroke when he changed the qualification system for the American team. His argument was that the points system used to determine the top 10 qualifiers over a period of two years did not allow for players who had amassed the majority of their points over the first 12 months losing form in the second year. He therefore called for the number of automatic qualifiers to be reduced to eight, which would grant him four wildcard selections instead of just two.

Azinger's request was granted and America's victory may have been the single most important development in safeguarding the immediate future of the Ryder Cup.

But, having rediscovered their appetite for the event, the United States have since suffered successive defeats by a single point at Celtic Manor, Wales and Medinah Country Club, Chicago, where Europe produced a stunning comeback in the singles to create the so-called "Miracle of Medinah."

While the USA has lost seven of the last nine matches, they were left kicking themselves in 2012 when they had victory in the palm of their hands and somehow let it slip away in a remarkable finale to the 39th contest.

Europe trailed 10-4 at one stage and had been written off with two fourball matches still on the course, and despite giving themselves a glimmer of hope by pulling the score back to 10-6 with the 12 single matches to be played, the odds were heavily in favour of a home victory.

But in one of the most remarkable days in the history of the Ryder Cup, Europe, led by Jose Maria Olazabal, somehow managed to win 8½ points to the Americans' 3½ to retain the trophy.

Germany's Martin Kaymer sank the putt against Steve Stricker that ensured a tied match and then Italian Francesco Molinari secured the final half-point by winning the 18th hole against Tiger Woods to halve his match and win the match outright.

Luke Donald, Ian Poulter, Rory McIlroy and Justin Rose led from the front, but it was generally agreed that Paul Lawrie's crushing 5&3 win over Brandt Snedeker had been the catalyst of the American's collapse, which was assisted by Sergio Garcia and Lee Westwood. ■

Ryder Cup Match Results

1927	Worcester Country Club, Massachusetts	USA 9½ GB 2½
1929	Moortown Golf Club, Leeds	GB 7 USA 5
1931	Scioto Country Club, Columbus, Ohio	USA 9 GB 3
1933	Southport & Ainsdale Golf Club, Southport	GB 6½ USA 5½
1935	Ridgewood Country Club, Ridgewood, New Jersey	USA 9 GB 3
1937	Southport & Ainsdale Golf Club, Southport	USA 8 GB 4
1947	Portland Golf Club, Portland, Oregon	USA 11 GB 1
1949	Ganton Golf Club, Scarborough	USA 7 GB 5
1951	Pinehurst Country Club, Pinehurst, North Carolina	USA 9½ GB 2½
1953	Wentworth Golf Club, Surrey	USA 6½ GB 5½
1955	Thunderbird Country Club, Palm Springs, California	USA 8 GB 4
1957	Lindrick Golf Club, Yorkshire	GB 7½ USA 4½
1959	Eldorado Country Club, Palm Desert, California	USA 8½ GB 3½
1961	Royal Lytham & St Annes, St Annes	USA 14½ GB 9½
1963	East Lake Country Club, Atlanta, Georgia	USA 23 GB 9
1965	Royal Birkdale, Southport	USA 19½ GB 12½
1967	Champions Golf Club, Houston, Texas	USA 23½ GB 8½
1969	Royal Birkdale, Southport	GB 16 USA 16
1971	Old Warson Country Club, St Louis, Missouri	USA 18½ GB 13½
1973	Muirfield, Edinburgh	USA 19 GB&I 13
1975	Laurel Valley Golf Club, Ligonier, Pennsylvania	USA 21 GB&I 11
1977	Royal Lytham & St Annes, St Annes	USA 12½ GB&I 7½
1979	The Greenbrier, White Sulphur Springs, West Virginia	USA 17 EUR 11
1981	Walton Heath Golf Club, Surrey	USA 18½ EUR 9½
1983	PGA National Golf Club, Palm Beach Gardens, Florida	USA 14½ EUR 13½
1985	The Belfry, Sutton Coldfield	EUR 16½ USA 11½
1987	Muirfield Village, Dublin. Ohio	EUR 15 USA 13
1989	The Belfry, Sutton Coldfield	EUR 14 USA 14
1991	The Ocean Course, Kiawah Island, South Carolina	USA 14½ EUR 13½
1993	The Belfry, Sutton Coldfield	USA 15 EUR 13
1995	Oak Hill Country Club, Rochester, New York	EUR 14½ USA 13½
1997	Valderrrama Golf Club, Sotogrande, Spain	EUR 14½ USA 13½
1999	The Country Club, Brookline, Massachusetts	USA 14½ EUR 13½
2002	The Belfry, Sutton Coldfield	EUR 15½ USA 12½
2004	Oakland Hills Country Club, Bloomfield Township, Michigan	EUR 18½ USA 9½
2006	The K Club, County Kildare, Ireland	EUR 18½ USA 9½
2008	Valhalla Golf Club, Louisville, Kentucky	USA 16½ EUR 11½
2010	Celtic Manor Resort, Newport, Wales	EUR 14½ USA 13½
2012	Medinah Country Club, Chicago, Illinois	EUR 14½ USA 13½

Memorable Ryder Cup Matches... One Good, Two Bad

1969 (Royal Birkdale Golf Club, Southport. GB 16 USA 16)

In perhaps the most sporting act in the 87-year history of the Ryder Cup, Jack Nicklaus conceded a putt to Tony Jacklin on the 18th green which ensured the home side tied the match.

Their match was all-square playing the last when Jacklin faced a nerve-jangling two-foot putt for a half point. But rather than force the Englishman to putt under extreme pressure, Nicklaus picked up Jacklin's marker.

Both players had reached the green in two on the par-5 closing hole. Nicklaus then ran his eagle putt five feet past before sinking his return for birdie. Jacklin had left his eagle putt two feet short but still needed a four to tie the match.

However, with the Americans having already retained the trophy as holders, Nicklaus told Jacklin: "I don't think you would have missed that putt, but in these circumstances I would never give you the opportunity."

Nicklaus' gesture was warmly applauded by the watching galleries, but it did not go down well with his team-mates, who felt he should have forced Jacklin to make the putt as a miss would have given the Americans an outright win.

And U.S. captain Sam Snead publicly criticised Nicklaus, adding: "All the boys thought it was ridiculous to give him that putt. We went over there to win, not to be good ol' boys."

1991 (The Ocean Course, Kiawah Island, South Carolina. USA 14½ Europe 13½)

Dubbed "The War on the Shore", it developed into a bitter encounter after the hosts appeared to be deliberately disrespectful to the European team at the ceremonial opening dinner by showing two videos, one highlights of past matches featuring only Americans and the other of then–United States President George H.W. Bush cheering on the home side.

The bad feeling was further fuelled by a clash involving Paul Azinger and Seve Ballesteros, who already had history, having been involved in a rules dispute two years previously.

Azinger accused Ballesteros of gamesmanship when he kept clearing his throat while the American's playing partner in the opening foursomes, Chip Beck was playing his shots.

There was a further altercation when Azinger and Beck switched their balls in violation of the rules. When Ballesteros called the violation, Azinger replied that the Americans were not trying to cheat and Ballesteros responded by saying: "Oh no. Breaking the rules and cheating are two different things."

The violation was called too late for the referee to take action, but Ballesteros reportedly said after he and Jose Maria Olazabal had won 2&1: "The American team has 11 nice guys – and Paul Azinger!"

Corey Pavin, who went on to captain the United States in the 2010 match at Celtic Manor, also caused controversy by sporting a Desert Storm baseball cap in support of US troops fighting in Iraq.

1999 (The Country Club, Brookline, Massachusetts. USA 14½ Europe 13½)

Eight years after "The War on the Shore", the "Battle of Brookline" was another bloody affair for the Europeans, in particular Scotland's Colin Montgomerie, who was roundly abused by a section of the American crowd throughout the three days.

Monty was not the only one to complain. Mark James, the European captain, later described it as a "bear pit" and there were reports that a spectator even spat at the Englishman's wife.

But it was on the final day that the real drama unfolded as the home side fought back from 10-6 down heading into the singles to snatch a dramatic victory.

The outcome hinged on the result of the singles match between American Justin Leonard and Spaniard Jose Maria Olazabal. With the match tied, Leonard needed at least a half point by either winning one of the last two holes to clinch outright victory or finish all-square with Olazabal.

After Olazabal's second shot left him with a 22-foot putt, Leonard watched as his effort rolled away from the cup, leaving him with a 45-footer for birdie. Amazingly, under the most intense pressure, he sank his third shot to spark wild celebrations with team-mates, their wives and some fans running onto the green.

It was wholly inappropriate behaviour, given that Olazabal had still to putt to extend the match. Olazabal tried to regain his focus. However, he missed his difficult putt and the American team and officials celebrated once again, albeit in a slightly more orderly fashion.

Furious Sam Torrance, one of James' assistants, claimed in a television interview that a TV cameraman had stood on Olazabal's line while filming the initial invasion and following the match a number of the US team apologised for their behaviour. ∎

The Quirky World of Golf

MILLIONS of golf tales have been told over a drink at the 19th hole; some of them even true.

Part of the fun of the game is the post-match analysis which develops into a round of anecdotes, unusual facts, jokes and memorable one-liners.

Here is a brief selection of a few of the best of them.

TEMPER, temper...in 1942, during a tournament in Florida, Ky Laffoon was so angry he shot his putter!

Having three-putted the last, Laffoon walked straight to his car, opened the boot and pulled out a pistol before pumping three bullets into his blade, shouting: "Take that you son of a bitch!"

Fellow American Tommy Bolt was also prone to outbursts of golf rage, earning him the nickname "Thunderbolt."

Famous for hurling clubs, Bolt was also given to shaking his fist at the sky and challenging God to come down and "fight like a man."

Two-time major champion Tony Jacklin also claims that Bolt would regularly break wind while stood on the tee, often when his playing partners were in mid-swing.

On one occasion he even tied his putter to the bumper of his car and drove off - to teach it a lesson!

CBS and Golf Channel commentator and former European Tour star David Feherty is renowned for his one-liners delivered in a unique and colourful style, such as: "It would be easier to pick a broken nose, than a winner in that group."

Or: "That ball is so far left, Lassie couldn't find it if it was wrapped in bacon!"

Referring to Sir Nick Faldo's habit of marrying much younger women, Feherty quipped: "I am sorry he couldn't be here this week, he is attending the birth of his next wife."

Describing watching Americans Jim Furyk and Phil Mickelson playing golf, he declared: "Jim's swing looks like an octopus falling out of a tree and watching Phil play golf is like watching a drunk chasing a balloon near the edge of a cliff."

Commentating at the 2011 Masters, Feherty announced: "It's a glorious day at Augusta. The only way to ruin it would be to play golf" followed a short time later with: "That was a great shot – if they had put the pin there today!"

The legendary Gene Sarazen, winner of seven majors, used to say: "All men are created equal. I'm just one stroke better than the rest."

American sportswriter Jim Murray once claimed: "Any guy who would pass up the chance to see Sam Snead play golf would pull the shades driving past the Taj Mahal."

Tom Weiskopf, winner of the 1973 Open at Troon, said of Jack Nicklaus: "Jack knew he was going to beat you. You knew Jack was going to beat you. And Jack knew that you knew he was going to beat you."

Extrovert John Daly is a talented singer and guitarist in addition to being a two-time major winner and he once produced an album entitled "My Life", which included a track called "Ally my Exes wear Rolexes" in reference to the millions of dollars he has paid out in alimony.

Eccentric Swede Jesper Parnevik, the son of a comedian, tried a diet of volcanic dust and fruit. He also became famous for wearing the peak of his cap turned up to help improve his suntan.

Walter Hagen, one of the game's greatest showmen and a player of extraordinary talent, winning 11 majors at a time when there were only three to play for, used to say that he didn't want to be a millionaire, just live like one.

The flamboyant American also regularly unnerved opponents by walking onto the first tee and asking: "Who's going to be second, then?"

When Bernhard Langer won the German Open in 1981 he was the first German to do so after a wait of 70 years.

Royal Lytham and St Annes is the only Open Championship course in Britain or America which begins with a par-3.

Nowadays the top golfers earn millions of pounds every year, but the first tournament with prize-money of one million dollars didn't take place until 1981 when the top prize at Sun City, South Africa was $500,000.

In August 1981, Alastair Bell and his sister, Janet holed in one at the 18th at the Sidmouth Golf Club, South Devon - one after the other.

Due to a petrol shortage, caused by the Suez Crisis, the 1957 Open was transferred from Muirfield to St. Andrews, where the close proximity of the railway station cut down on reliance on cars and public transport by road.

A birdie, defined as a hole completed in one-under-par, originated in 1899 at Atlantic City Country Club when a member of a three-ball sent his second shot to within six inches of the cup at the par-4 second hole, describing it as a "bird of a shot."

Probably the best golfing movie was "Follow the Sun," based on the life of Ben Hogan and starring Glenn Ford in the lead role. It was released in 1951, the year Hogan successfully defended the US Open and two years after the car crash that very nearly cost him his life.

There have been a number of attempts by Hollywood to produce a golf Oscar-winner without success, including Bob Hope in "Call Me Bwana" in which Arnold Palmer appeared in a cameo role.

There have been two sets of father and son winners of the Open – Willie Park, Senior and Willie Park, Junior and Old Tom Morris and Young Tom Morris.

Percy Alliss and son Peter, the noted television commentator, both played for Great Britain in the Ryder Cup and the brothers Bernard and Geoffrey Hunt were members of the 1963 team. Siblings Charles, Ernest and Reg Whitcombe also achieved the feat.

In the 1960 Open at St Andrews Gary Player wore trousers with one black leg and one white to protest against apartheid.

According to Tiger Woods, hockey is a sport for white men. Basketball is a sport for black men while golf is a sport for white men dressed like black pimps!

The late Dean Martin, who enjoyed lubricating his vocal chords with a drop or two of the hard stuff, had this advice for fellow drinkers, "If you drink, don't drive. Don't even putt!"

The writer P.G Wodehouse believed that the best way to find out a man's true character was to play golf with him.

And former US President Gerald Ford, prone to a series of mishaps on the golf course, claimed, "I know I am getting better at golf because I am hitting fewer spectators!" ■

Date	Name	Venue	Score		Date	Name
1860	Willie Park, Sr.	Prestwick	174 (36)		1909	John Henry Taylor
1861	Tom Morris, Sr.	Prestwick	163		1910	James Braid
1862	Tom Morris, Sr.	Prestwick	163		1911	Harry Vardon
1863	Willie Park, Sr.	Prestwick	168		1912	Ted Ray
1864	Tom Morris, Sr.	Prestwick	167		1913	John Henry Taylor
1865	Andrew Strath	Prestwick	162		1914	Harry Vardon
1866	Willie Park, Sr.	Prestwick	169		1920	George Duncan
1867	Tom Morris, Sr.	Prestwick	170		1921	Jock Hutchison (USA)
1868	Tom Morris, Jr.	Prestwick	154		1922	Walter Hagen (USA)
1869	Tom Morris, Jr.	Prestwick	157		1923	Arthur Havers
1870	Tom Morris, Jr.	Prestwick	149		1924	Walter Hagen (USA)
1872	Tom Morris, Jr.	Prestwick	166		1925	Jim Barnes
1873	Tom Kidd	St Andrews	179		1926	Bobby Jones † (USA)
1874	Mungo Park	Musselburgh	159		1927	Bobby Jones † (USA)
1875	Willie Park, Sr.	Prestwick	166		1928	Walter Hagen (USA)
1876	Bob Martin	St Andrews	176		1929	Walter Hagen (USA)
1877	Jamie Anderson	Musselburgh	160		1930	Bobby Jones † (USA)
1878	Jamie Anderson	Prestwick	157		1931	Tommy Armour (USA)
1879	Jamie Anderson	St Andrews	169		1932	Gene Sarazen (USA)
1880	Bob Ferguson	Musselburgh	162		1933	Denny Shute (USA)
1881	Bob Ferguson	Prestwick	170		1934	Henry Cotton
1882	Bob Ferguson	St Andrews	171		1935	Alf Perry
1883	Willie Fernie	Musselburgh	159		1936	Alf Padgham
1884	Jack Simpson	Prestwick	160		1937	Henry Cotton
1885	Bob Martin	St Andrews	171		1938	Reg Whitcombe
1886	David Brown	Musselburgh	157		1939	Dick Burton
1887	Willie Park, Jr.	Prestwick	161		1946	Sam Snead (USA)
1888	Jack Burns	St Andrews	171		1947	Fred Daly
1889	Willie Park, Jr.	Musselburgh	155		1948	Henry Cotton
1890	John Ball, Jr. †	Prestwick	164		1949	Bobby Locke (RSA)
1891	Hugh Kirkaldy	St Andrews	166		1950	Bobby Locke (RSA)
1892	Harold H Hilton †	Muirfield	305 (72)		1951	Max Faulkner
1893	William Auchterlonie	Prestwick	322		1952	Bobby Locke (RSA)
1894	John Henry Taylor	Royal St George's	326		1953	Ben Hogan (USA)
1895	John Henry Taylor	St Andrews	332		1954	Peter Thomson (AUS)
1896	Harry Vardon	Muirfield	316		1955	Peter Thomson (AUS)
1897	Harold H Hilton †	Royal Liverpool	314		1956	Peter Thomson (AUS)
1898	Harry Vardon	Prestwick	307		1957	Bobby Locke (RSA)
1899	Harry Vardon	Royal St George's	310		1958	Peter Thomson (AUS)
1900	John Henry Taylor	St Andrews	309		1959	Gary Player (RSA)
1901	James Braid	Muirfield	309		1960	Kel Nagle (AUS)
1902	Sandy Herd	Royal Liverpool	307		1961	Arnold Palmer (USA)
1903	Harry Vardon	Prestwick	300		1962	Arnold Palmer (USA)
1904	Jack White	Royal St George's	296		1963	Bob Charles (NZL)
1905	James Braid	St Andrews	318		1964	Tony Lema (USA)
1906	James Braid	Muirfield	300		1965	Peter Thomson (AUS)
1907	Arnaud Massy (FRA)	Royal Liverpool	312		1966	Jack Nicklaus (USA)
1908	James Braid	Prestwick	291		1967	Roberto DeVicenzo (ARG)

Venue	Score
Royal Cinque Ports	291
St Andrews	299
Royal St George's	303
Muirfield	295
Royal Liverpool	304
Prestwick	306
Royal Cinque Ports	303
St Andrews	296
Royal St George's	300
Royal Troon	295
Royal Liverpool	301
Prestwick	300
Royal Lytham & St Annes	291
St Andrews	285
Royal St George's	292
Muirfield	292
Royal Liverpool	291
Carnoustie	296
Prince's Golf Club	283
St Andrews	292
Royal St George's	283
Muirfield	283
Royal Liverpool	287
Carnoustie	290
Royal St George's	295
St Andrews	290
St Andrews	290
Royal Liverpool	293
Muirfield	284
Royal St George's	283
Royal Troon	279
Royal Portrush	285
Royal Lytham & St Annes	287
Carnoustie	282
Royal Birkdale	283
St Andrews	281
Royal Liverpool	286
St Andrews	279
Royal Lytham & St Annes	274
Muirfield	284
St Andrews	278
Royal Birkdale	284
Royal Troon	276
Royal Lytham & St Annes	277
St Andrews	279
Royal Birkdale	285
Muirfield	282
Royal Liverpool	278

Date	Name	Venue	Score
1968	Gary Player (RSA)	Carnoustie	289
1969	Tony Jacklin	Royal Lytham & St Annes	280
1970	Jack Nicklaus (USA)	St Andrews	283
1971	Lee Trevino (USA)	Royal Birkdale	278
1972	Lee Trevino (USA)	Muirfield	278
1973	Tom Weiskopf (USA)	Royal Troon	276
1974	Gary Player (RSA)	Royal Lytham & St Annes	282
1975	Tom Watson (USA)	Carnoustie	279
1976	Johnny Miller (USA)	Royal Birkdale	279
1977	Tom Watson (USA)	Turnberry	268
1978	Jack Nicklaus (USA)	St Andrews	281
1979	Seve Ballesteros (ESP)	Royal Lytham & St Annes	283
1980	Tom Watson (USA)	Muirfield	271
1981	Bill Rogers (USA)	Royal St George's	276
1982	Tom Watson (USA)	Royal Troon	284
1983	Tom Watson (USA)	Royal Birkdale	275
1984	Seve Ballesteros (ESP)	St Andrews	276
1985	Sandy Lyle	Royal St George's	282
1986	Greg Norman (AUS)	Turnberry	280
1987	Sir Nick Faldo	Muirfield	279
1988	Seve Ballesteros (ESP)	Royal Lytham & St Annes	273
1989	Mark Calcavecchia (USA)	Royal Troon	275
1990	Sir Nick Faldo	St Andrews	270
1991	Ian Baker-Finch (AUS)	Royal Birkdale	272
1992	Sir Nick Faldo	Muirfield	272
1993	Greg Norman (AUS)	Royal St George's	267
1994	Nick Price (ZIM)	Turnberry	268
1995	John Daly (USA)	St Andrews	282
1996	Tom Lehman (USA)	Royal Lytham & St Annes	271
1997	Justin Leonard (USA)	Royal Troon	272
1998	Mark O'Meara (USA)	Royal Birkdale	280
1999	Paul Lawrie	Carnoustie	290
2000	Tiger Woods (USA)	St Andrews	269
2001	David Duval (USA)	Royal Lytham & St Annes	274
2002	Ernie Els (RSA)	Muirfield	278
2003	Ben Curtis (USA)	Royal St George's	283
2004	Todd Hamilton (USA)	Royal Troon	274
2005	Tiger Woods (USA)	St Andrews	274
2006	Tiger Woods (USA)	Royal Liverpool	270
2007	Pádraig Harrington (IRL)	Carnoustie	277
2008	Pádraig Harrington (IRL)	Royal Birkdale	283
2009	Stewart Cink (USA)	Turnberry	278
2010	Louis Oosthuizen (RSA)	St Andrews	272
2011	Darren Clarke	Royal St George's	275
2012	Ernie Els (RSA)	Royal Lytham & St Annes	273
2013	Phil Mickelson (USA)	Muirfield	281

† Amateur   GB Unless Stated   1915-1919 Not Played (World War I)   1940-1945 Not Played (World War II)

The Leaderboard Stats

Date	Name	Score
1934	Horton Smith	284
1935	Gene Sarazen	282
1936	Horton Smith	285
1937	Byron Nelson	283
1938	Henry Picard	285
1939	Ralph Guldahl	279
1940	Jimmy Demaret	280
1941	Craig Wood	280
1942	Byron Nelson	280
1946	Herman Keiser	282
1947	Jimmy Demaret	281
1948	Claude Harmon	279
1949	Sam Snead	282
1950	Jimmy Demaret	283
1951	Ben Hogan	280
1952	Sam Snead	286
1953	Ben Hogan	274
1954	Sam Snead	289
1955	Cary Middlecoff	279
1956	Jack Burke, Jr.	289
1957	Doug Ford	283
1958	Arnold Palmer	284
1959	Art Wall, Jr.	284
1960	Arnold Palmer	282
1961	Gary Player (RSA)	280
1962	Arnold Palmer	280
1963	Jack Nicklaus	286
1964	Arnold Palmer	276
1965	Jack Nicklaus	271
1966	Jack Nicklaus	288
1967	Gay Brewer	280
1968	Bob Goalby	277
1969	George Archer	281
1970	Billy Casper	279
1971	Charles Coody	279
1972	Jack Nicklaus	286
1973	Tommy Aaron	283
1974	Gary Player (RSA)	278
1975	Jack Nicklaus	276
1976	Raymond Floyd	271

© George Tiedemann/Corbis

Masters Tournament

Seve wins in 1983.

Date	Name	Score
1977	Tom Watson	276
1978	Gary Player (RSA)	277
1979	Fuzzy Zoeller	280
1980	Seve Ballesteros (ESP)	275
1981	Tom Watson	280
1982	Craig Stadler	284
1983	Seve Ballesteros (ESP)	280
1984	Ben Crenshaw	277
1985	Bernhard Langer (GER)	282
1986	Jack Nicklaus	279
1987	Larry Mize	285
1988	Sandy Lyle (SCO)	281
1989	Sir Nick Faldo (ENG)	283
1990	Sir Nick Faldo (ENG)	278
1991	Ian Woosnam (WAL)	277
1992	Fred Couples	275
1993	Bernhard Langer (GER)	277
1994	José María Olazábal (ESP)	279
1995	Ben Crenshaw	274
1996	Sir Nick Faldo (ENG)	276
1997	Tiger Woods	270
1998	Mark O'Meara	279
1999	José María Olazábal (ESP)	280
2000	Vijay Singh (FIJ)	278
2001	Tiger Woods	272
2002	Tiger Woods	276
2003	Mike Weir (CAN)	281
2004	Phil Mickelson	279
2005	Tiger Woods	276
2006	Phil Mickelson	281
2007	Zach Johnson	289
2008	Trevor Immelman (RSA)	280
2009	Ángel Cabrera (ARG)	276
2010	Phil Mickelson	272
2011	Charl Schwartzel (RSA)	274
2012	Bubba Watson	278
2013	Adam Scott (AUS)	279
2014	Bubba Watson	280

American Unless Stated   1943-1945 Not Played (World War II)

The Leaderboard Stats

Date	Name	Venue	Score	Date	Name
1895	Horace Rawlins (ENG)	Newport	173	1939	Byron Nelson
1896	James Foulis (SCO)	Shinnecock Hills	152	1940	Lawson Little
1897	Joe Lloyd (ENG)	Chicago	162	1941	Craig Wood
1898	Fred Herd (SCO)	Myopia Hunt Club	328	1946	Lloyd Mangrum
1899	Willie Smith (SCO)	Baltimore	315	1947	Lew Worsham
1900	Harry Vardon (ENG)	Chicago	313	1948	Ben Hogan
1901	Willie Anderson (SCO)	Myopia Hunt Club	331	1949	Cary Middlecoff
1902	Laurie Auchterlonie (SCO)	Garden City	307	1950	Ben Hogan
1903	Willie Anderson (SCO)	Baltusrol	307	1951	Ben Hogan
1904	Willie Anderson (SCO)	Glen View	303	1952	Julius Boros
1905	Willie Anderson (SCO)	Myopia Hunt Club	314	1953	Ben Hogan
1906	Alex Smith (SCO)	Onwentsia	295	1954	Ed Furgol
1907	Alec Ross (SCO)	Philadelphia Cricket Club	302	1955	Jack Fleck
1908	Fred McLeod (SCO)	Myopia Hunt Club	322		
1909	George Sargent (ENG)	Englewood	290	1956	Cary Middlecoff
1910	Alex Smith (SCO)	Philadelphia Cricket Club	298	1957	Dick Mayer
1911	John McDermott	Chicago	307	1958	Tommy Bolt
1912	John McDermott	CC of Buffalo	294	1959	Billy Casper
1913	Francis Ouimet †	The Country Club	304	1960	Arnold Palmer
1914	Walter Hagen	Midlothian	290	1961	Gene Littler
1915	Jerome Travers †	Baltusrol	297	1962	Jack Nicklaus
1916	Chick Evans †	Minikahda	286	1963	Julius Boros
1919	Walter Hagen	Brae Burn	301	1964	Ken Venturi
1920	Ted Ray (ENG)	Inverness	295	1965	Gary Player (RSA)
1921	Jim Barnes (ENG)	Columbia	289	1966	Billy Casper
1922	Gene Sarazen	Skokie	288		
1923	Bobby Jones †	Inwood	296	1967	Jack Nicklaus
1924	Cyril Walker (ENG)	Oakland Hills	297	1968	Lee Trevino
1925	Willie Macfarlane (SCO)	Worcester	291	1969	Orville Moody
1926	Bobby Jones †	Scioto	293	1970	Tony Jacklin (ENG)
1927	Tommy Armour (SCO)	Oakmont	301	1971	Lee Trevino
1928	Johnny Farrell	Olympia Fields	294	1972	Jack Nicklaus
1929	Bobby Jones †	Winged Foot	294	1973	Johnny Miller
1930	Bobby Jones †	Interlachen	287	1974	Hale Irwin
1931	Billy Burke	Inverness	292	1975	Lou Graham
1932	Gene Sarazen	Fresh Meadows	286	1976	Jerry Pate
1933	Johnny Goodman †	North Shore	287		
1934	Olin Dutra	Merion Cricket Club	293	1977	Hubert Green
1935	Sam Parks, Jr.	Oakmont	299	1978	Andy North
1936	Tony Manero	Baltusrol	282	1979	Hale Irwin
1937	Ralph Guldahl	Oakland Hills	281	1980	Jack Nicklaus
1938	Ralph Guldahl	Cherry Hills	284	1981	David Graham (AUS)

US Open Championship

Venue	Score
Philadelphia	284
Canterbury	287
Colonial	284
Canterbury	284
St. Louis	282
Riviera	276
Medinah	286
Merion (East Course)	287
Oakland Hills	287
Northwood	281
Oakmont	283
Baltusrol	284
Olympic Club (Lake Course)	287
Oak Hill (East Course)	281
Inverness	282
Southern Hills	283
Winged Foot	282
Cherry Hills	280
Oakland Hills	281
Oakmont	283
The Country Club	293
Congressional	278
Bellerive	282
Olympic Club (Lake Course)	278
Baltusrol	275
Oak Hill (East Course)	275
Champions	281
Hazeltine National	281
Merion (East Course)	280
Pebble Beach	290
Oakmont	279
Winged Foot Golf Club	287
Medinah	287
Atlanta Athletic Club (Highlands Course)	277
Southern Hills	278
Cherry Hills	285
Inverness	284
Baltusrol	272
Merion (East Course)	273

Date	Name	Venue	Score
1982	Tom Watson	Pebble Beach	282
1983	Larry Nelson	Oakmont	280
1984	Fuzzy Zoeller	Winged Foot	276
1985	Andy North	Oakland Hills	279
1986	Raymond Floyd	Shinnecock Hills	279
1987	Scott Simpson	Olympic Club (Lake Course)	277
1988	Curtis Strange	The Country Club	278
1989	Curtis Strange	Oak Hill (East Course)	278
1990	Hale Irwin	Medinah	280
1991	Payne Stewart	Hazeltine National	282
1992	Tom Kite	Pebble Beach	285
1993	Lee Janzen	Baltusrol	272
1994	Ernie Els (RSA)	Oakmont	279
1995	Corey Pavin	Shinnecock Hills	280
1996	Steve Jones	Oakland Hills	278
1997	Ernie Els (RSA)	Congressional (Blue Course)	276
1998	Lee Janzen	Olympic Club (Lake Course)	280
1999	Payne Stewart	Pinehurst (No. 2)	279
2000	Tiger Woods	Pebble Beach	272
2001	Retief Goosen (RSA)	Southern Hills	276
2002	Tiger Woods	Bethpage State Park (Black Course)	277
2003	Jim Furyk	Olympia Fields	272
2004	Retief Goosen (RSA)	Shinnecock Hills	276
2005	Michael Campbell (NZL)	Pinehurst (No. 2)	280
2006	Geoff Ogilvy (AUS)	Winged Foot	285
2007	Ángel Cabrera (ARG)	Oakmont	285
2008	Tiger Woods	Torrey Pines	283
2009	Lucas Glover	Bethpage State Park (Black Course)	276
2010	Graeme McDowell (NIR)	Pebble Beach	284
2011	Rory McIlroy (NIR)	Congressional (Blue Course)	268
2012	Webb Simpson	Olympic Club (Lake Course)	281
2013	Justin Rose (ENG)	Merion (East Course)	281

† Amateur   American Unless Stated   1917-1918 Not Played (World War I)   1942-1945 Not Played (World War II)

Gene Sarazen.

Date	Name
1933	Gene Sarazen
1934	Paul Runyan
1935	Johnny Revolta
1936	Denny Shute
1937	Denny Shute
1938	Paul Runyan
1939	Henry Picard
1940	Byron Nelson
1941	Vic Ghezzi
1942	Sam Snead
1944	Bob Hamilton
1945	Byron Nelson
1946	Ben Hogan
1947	Jim Ferrier (AUS)
1948	Ben Hogan
1949	Sam Snead
1950	Chandler Harper
1951	Sam Snead
1952	Jim Turnesa
1953	Walter Burkemo
1954	Chick Harbert
1955	Doug Ford
1956	Jack Burke, Jr.
1957	Lionel Hebert

Date	Name
1958	Dow Finsterwald
1959	Bob Rosburg
1960	Jay Hebert
1961	Jerry Barber
1962	Gary Player (RSA)
1963	Jack Nicklaus
1964	Bobby Nichols
1965	Dave Marr
1966	Al Geiberger
1967	Don January
1968	Julius Boros
1969	Raymond Floyd
1970	Dave Stockton
1971	Jack Nicklaus
1972	Gary Player(RSA)
1973	Jack Nicklaus
1974	Lee Trevino
1975	Jack Nicklaus

Date	Name	Venue	Margin
1916	Jim Barnes (ENG)	Siwanoy	1 up
1919	Jim Barnes (ENG)	Engineers	6 & 5
1920	Jock Hutchison (SCO)	Flossmoor	1 up
1921	Walter Hagen	Inwood	3 & 2
1922	Gene Sarazen	Oakmont	4 & 3
1923	Gene Sarazen	Pelham	38 holes
1924	Walter Hagen	French Lick	2 up
1925	Walter Hagen	Olympia Fields	6 & 5
1926	Walter Hagen	Salisbury	5 & 3
1927	Walter Hagen	Cedar Crest	1 up
1928	Leo Diegel	Baltimore	6 & 5
1929	Leo Diegel	Hillcrest	6 & 4
1930	Tommy Armour (SCO)	Fresh Meadow	1 up
1931	Tom Creavy	Wannamoisett	2 & 1
1932	Olin Dutra	Keller	4 & 3

Venue	Margin
Blue Mound	5 & 4
Park	38 holes
Twin Hills	5 & 4
Pinehurst	3 & 2
Pittsburgh	37 holes
Shawnee	8 & 7
Pomonok	37 holes
Hershey	1 up
Cherry Hills	38 holes
Seaview	2 & 1
Manito	1 up
Moraine	4 & 3
Portland	6 & 4
Plum Hollow	2 & 1
Norwood Hills	7 & 6
Hermitage	3 & 2
Scioto	4 & 3
Oakmont	7 & 6
Big Spring	1 up
Birmingham	2 & 1
Keller	4 & 3
Meadowbrook	4 & 3
Blue Hill	3 & 2
Miami Valley	2 & 1

Venue	Score
Llanerch	276
Minneapolis	277
Firestone	281
Olympia Fields	277
Aronimink	278
Dallas Athletic Club	279
Columbus	271
Laurel Valley	280
Firestone	280
Columbine	281
Pecan Valley	281
NCR CC	276
Southern Hills	279
PGA National	281
Oakland Hills	281
Canterbury	277
Tanglewood	276
Firestone	276

Date	Name	Venue	Score
1976	Dave Stockton	Congressional	281
1977	Lanny Wadkins	Pebble Beach	282
1978	John Mahaffey	Oakmont	276
1979	David Graham(AUS)	Oakland Hills	272
1980	Jack Nicklaus	Oak Hill, East Course	274
1981	Larry Nelson	Atlanta Athletic Club, Highlands Course	273
1982	Raymond Floyd	Southern Hills	272
1983	Hal Sutton	Riviera	274
1984	Lee Trevino	Shoal Creek	273
1985	Hubert Green	Cherry Hills	278
1986	Bob Tway	Inverness	276
1987	Larry Nelson	PGA National	287
1988	Jeff Sluman	Oak Tree	272
1989	Payne Stewart	Kemper Lakes	276
1990	Wayne Grady (AUS)	Shoal Creek	282
1991	John Daly	Crooked Stick	276
1992	Nick Price (ZIM)	Bellerive	278
1993	Paul Azinger	Inverness	272
1994	Nick Price (ZIM)	Southern Hills	269
1995	Steve Elkington (AUS)	Riviera	267
1996	Mark Brooks	Valhalla	277
1997	Davis Love III	Winged Foot	269
1998	Vijay Singh (FIJ)	Sahalee	271
1999	Tiger Woods	Medinah, No. 3	277
2000	Tiger Woods	Valhalla	270
2001	David Toms	Atlanta Athletic Club, Highlands Course	265
2002	Rich Beem	Hazeltine	278
2003	Shaun Micheel	Oak Hill, East Course	276
2004	Vijay Singh (FIJ)	Whistling Straits	280
2005	Phil Mickelson	Baltusrol, Lower Course	276
2006	Tiger Woods	Medinah, No. 3	270
2007	Tiger Woods	Southern Hills	272
2008	Pádraig Harrington (IRL)	Oakland Hills	277
2009	Yang Yong-eun (KOR)	Hazeltine	280
2010	Martin Kaymer (GER)	Whistling Straits	277
2011	Keegan Bradley	Atlanta Athletic Club, Highlands Course	272
2012	Rory McIlroy (NIR)	Kiawah Island, Ocean Course	275
2013	Jason Dufner	Oak Hill, East Course	270

American Unless Stated   Until 1957 the Championship was decided by match play
1917-1918 Not Played (World War I)   1943 Not Played (World War II)

My Magnificent Obsession

John Millar

it was NEARLY another hole in one at the par 3 18th hole at Ardeer in June 2013.

Recovering from major heart surgery John Millar took his wife's advice to get more exercise. In his late 50s he took up golf for the first time.

LIKE others who had never bothered to step on to a tee, I had supported the view that golf was a good walk spoiled. Just goes to show how wrong you can be.

But it took years to shake off my pig-headed attitude before finally summoning up the will and determination to plunge head-long into the mysteries, and often dark arts, of the world of golf.

The reasons for steadfastly refusing to consider the game had been many. My Dad – now a remarkable 91 years old – was a good player and who would want to be beaten by a geriatric, even if he is your flesh and blood! Co-ordination and I are not old acquaintances and I only have one fully functioning eye, so making the correct contact between club and ball was always going to be a minor miracle.

I could go on and on down the lists of reasons to be fearful but it would sound too much like moaning. Anyway it seemed perfectly clear that golf was never, ever going to be on my to-do list. But, as Sean Connery – who knows his way round quite a few golf courses – advised us...never say never.

My road to Damascus moment came in my late fifties when, after having had heart surgery a few years earlier, my wife was anxious that I should take on some form of regular exercise.

I'd tried walking. Boring. Jogging was a non-starter. The guy who invented it died of a heart attack. Didn't fancy swimming. Too wet. So what about golf? I'd won a golf bag in a raffle (fate or what?) and, after getting a second-hand set of clubs, thought I'd give it a go.

This was not an overnight success story. I was not a natural. Indeed when my Dad witnessed my first efforts he offered this sage observation..."You are not the worst golfer I've ever seen, son...but pretty close."

He was not being cruel. I was dreadful. Too old to learn. Too stiff to have the physical flexibility needed. My visits to the golf course must have appeared as though I was trying to emulate the TV treks of David Attenborough as I waded deep into knee-high jungle rough and burrowed through small forests in search of yet another errant wee white ball.

All of which should have been so discouraging that I'd chuck the clubs away and bid a not very fond farewell to the fairways and greens – none of which I'd got to know as well as the seemingly endless acres of unforgiving rough.

Strangely though, giving up never crossed my mind. As hopeless as I was, I was hooked. Almost

instantly golf became a magnificent obsession. I even started to adopt – and sometimes actually understand – golf jargon. Proof, if needed, that I was a golf addict came when very brightly coloured shirts and trousers began to dominate my wardrobe.

Remarkably I got better. Never brilliant. Ok, sometimes bordering on adequate. And, wonder of wonders, I fluked a hole in one. Not once but twice. Naturally those lucky, lucky golf balls are framed and have pride of place in my study.

Even though I did not see either of those shots go straight from tee to hole – I can rarely follow the flight of the ball – they are golden memories. As are the times when I was fortunate enough to be a guest at glorious and so very different courses that range from Loch Lomond and St Andrews to the Dordogne and Los Angeles.

Recollections of those rounds are varied. Hitting just about every water hazard at Loch Lomond, shivering as a biting Easterly wind blew across Fife and recovering from some horrible shots by chipping in for a birdie on the Black Perigord.

The most cherished memory came after duffing my way round the Rancho Park course in the early morning Californian sunshine. At a par-5 hole my attention was drawn to a plaque that reminds us that even legends can be humbled by the wonderful, infuriating game of golf.

That plaque does not commemorate a classic score or a wonder shot. It is a marker for one of the great abberations in golfing history. Its source goes way back to 1961, during the playing of the LA Open, at a time when Arnold Palmer was the PGA Golfer of the Year. But even a great like Arnie can have a disastrous hole. And Arnie did!

After a decent drive he sliced two shots into the driving range before hooking another two into the street that runs alongside the fairway. He then hit on to the green and two putted. Eight strokes and four penalties for a 12!

So, after absorbing the details of this nightmare hole, I rather nervously hit off and somehow – I still can't explain it – scrambled a six! I'd managed to halve Arnie's infamous score and felt like a king.

Suddenly all the mishits of the round had evaporated from my mind as I gloried in an experience that I knew wouldn't be repeated very often. It will also not have escaped notice that my game is such that I regard a bogey as a success. But grab the scraps where and when you can.

Though I am keenly aware that any golden bits of play will always be far, far outweighed by the multitude of horrors that lie in wait out there on the fairways...the shank, the slice, three to get out a bunker, the missed one foot putt...all that doesn't seem to matter. I have discovered a game that, perversely perhaps, gives me a lot of joy. The trick, I assume, is to follow the wisdom of Rudyard Kipling and treat triumph and disaster as equally inconsequential imposters.

Oh yes and enjoy the next occasion in which you manage to manufacture something that feels approximately like a real golf shot. ■